THE ELEMENTS OF MEDITATION

Dr David Fontana is Reader in Educational Psychology at the University of Wales, Cardiff. He is the author of a number of highly acclaimed books in psychology and has spent many years in both personal and professional study of the psychological and spiritual benefits of meditation, learning from both Eastern and Western teachers. His best-selling *Dreamlife: Understanding and Using Your Dreams* is also published by Element.

The *Elements Of* is a series designed to present high quality introductions to a broad range of essential subjects.

The books are commissioned specifically from experts in their fields. They provide readable and often unique views of the various topics covered, and are therefore of interest both to those who have some knowledge of the subject, as well as those who are approaching it for the first time.

Many of these concise yet comprehensive books have practical suggestions and exercises which allow personal experiences as well as theoretical understanding, and offer a valuable source of information on many important themes.

In the same series

THE ELEMENTS OF

MEDITATION

David Fontana

ELEMENT

Shaftesbury, Dorset ● Rockport, Massachusetts
Brisbane, Queensland

© David Fontana 1991

Published in Great Britain in 1991 by
Element Books Limited
Longmead, Shaftesbury, Dorset

Published in the USA in 1991 by
Element, Inc.
42 Broadway, Rockport, MA 01966

Reprinted 1992
Reprinted 1993

Published in Australia by
Element Books Ltd for
Jacaranda Wiley Ltd,
33 Park Road, Milton, Brisbane, 4064

Cover illustration by Barbara McGavin
Cover design by Max Fairbrother and Barbara McGavin
Typeset by Selectmove Ltd, London
Printed and bound in Great Britain by
Biddles Ltd, Guildford & King's Lynn

British Library Cataloguing in Publication Data
Fontana, David
The elements of meditation.
I. Title
158.12

Library of Congress data available

ISBN 1–85230–229–1

Contents

ACKNOWLEDGEMENTS

Dedicating this book to any of those who have helped my meditation practices might be presumptious, in that it would imply their support for all I have written. This would be inappropriate. Instead I gratefully acknowledge their wisdom, in particular that of John Crook, Lama Damcho Yonten, Lama Yeshe Dorje, Lama Chhimed Rigdzin Rinpoche, Lama Sogyal Rinpoche, Ngakpa Chögyam, Reverend Master Daishin Morgan, Godwin Sararatne, Manny Patel, and Flo Farmer. And since books have been so important in my life, I feel honoured also to acknowledge those teachers like Eugen Herrigel, Lama Govinda, John Blofeld and Charles Luk who I never met, but who are nevertheless intimate friends.

1 · BEGINNING THE JOURNEY

MANY WAYS OF TRAVELLING

There are many ways of travelling. When we are very small we travel by crawling. Then we learn to stand and to take our first few steps. Then we learn to walk, looking the world in the face and learning something of its moods, happy and sad. Later, we take to bicycles, and then to cars and trains and boats and even to aeroplanes, moving with the speed of sound and shrinking the world below us like a deflated balloon. Distances which to our ancestors would have seemed unimaginable disappear without thought. In the modern world, so much of our life is bound up with movement. We rarely stay for long in the same place. With a kind of restless energy we devour time and space, forever just passing through, forever on the way to somewhere else, forever in transit, forever with our bags packed and our coats on, ready to depart.

But there is another way of travelling. A way of travelling that begins when we first open our eyes on the world, and that continues until we draw our last breath. An inner way of travelling that carries us through the scenery of our own minds. A journey made not by boats and planes but by thoughts and feelings, by the constant play of our own inner experience. A journey which embraces alike the routine progress of daily

1

life and the magical flights of imagination that take us to the moon or back to the dawn of time. A journey that transports us through a vast sweep of feelings and emotions, from dizzy heights to bitter depths. A journey that we have no option but to take, since it is the journey of being alive, of being who we are.

Stop reading for a moment and just think about this journey. Close your eyes. Experience for a moment the sensation of being alive, of being in your own mind, undistracted by outer events, unhindered by the world of hearing and seeing. . . how did that feel? Usually we are so occupied by the world out there that we never stop to think that reality is what happens in here. The outer world, that supposedly solid and objective world of colours and shapes and people and objects only has existence for us when we have registered it in here, when it has passed through the filter of our senses and been recognized and interpreted by our own minds.

We become so used to this recognition and interpretation that we forget it's happening. We forget that things have no reality for us until we've internalized them. We rarely attend directly to our minds, to the inner world of our own being. Our attention is forever turned outwards, as if the objects around us create our experience independently of us ourselves, as if our experience of life is conjured into being by outer magic rather than by our own senses and the enchantment of our own minds.

LOST IN THOUGHT

'But', you may argue, 'I'm always attending to my mind. That's half my trouble. I'm constantly lost in thought instead of concentrating on what I'm supposed to be doing.' Yes all right. But to be lost in thought is simply attending to mental chatter, to the train of associations that starts at one point and meanders off into the distance until we can't even remember where our starting point was. This isn't attending to your mind. It's surrendering control to an inner monologue so dominating that it forces unwanted thoughts on us and insists we attend to them whether we like it or not. An inner monologue that goads us constantly into returning to our worries, our depressions,

2

our jealousies, our grievances, our hostilities. A monologue that allows us to recall happy memories one moment, only to sadden us the next by reminding us that those happy times are past. A monologue that prompts us to dream up imaginary disasters, to go over and over a bruising encounter we've just had with someone, to rehearse endlessly what we should have said to them if only we'd thought of it in time. A monologue that has us so completely at its mercy that one is prompted to ask, 'Who's in charge in here?'

The same lack of control applies to our feelings. Emotions arise whether we want them to or not. We feel happy or sad, angry or frightened, contented or discontented, attracted or repelled, patient or impatient, interested or bored, as if we have no say at all in the matter. If we stop to think about it, we have to admit that much of the time these emotions seem to rise and fall with a will of their own, as independent of us as the coming and going of day and night.

But there's worse than this. For even when our attention is directed outwards, for most of the time we aren't properly attending at all. Our attention is pulled first one way and then another. We look at or listen to something and then almost immediately switch to looking at or listening to something else. We start a job and break off half-way through as other demands press in upon us. We try to do umpteen things at once. We have an object in our hands, put it down, and a moment later can't remember where we've put it. We hear something and a moment later we've forgotten what it was. Our minds flit from one thing to another like demented butterflies. And then, to crown it all, we blame our inefficiency upon our poor memories, or upon other people or upon the circumstances of our hectic and fragmented lives.

Does it have to be like this? Are we constructed in such a way that our minds – and thus much of our lives – must forever remain outside our control and, equally importantly, our understanding? Or is there a way in which we can take over at least some of this control and gain at least some of this understanding – and become in the process more in touch with who we really are? For without self-control and self-understanding, we are destined in a real sense to stay strangers to ourselves, as if we have inside us a wilful and unpredictable child who pays no heed to our wishes and insists on going his or her own way even when it's clear that way leads to disaster.

TRANSFORMING THE JOURNEY

The answer is that no, it doesn't have to be like this; and yes, there is a way in which we can take more charge and develop more understanding of what goes on *in here*, and become more our own man or woman. Which brings me back full circle to the notion of travelling. We are already engaged on the journey of experiencing our own lives, but what we can do – if we so wish – is take the direction of that journey into our own hands, and take more of our own decisions as to the path we follow and as to how we travel it. If we wish – and the choice is always our own – we can begin to transform the journey from one of confusion to one of clarity, rather like washing the sleep from our eyes and seeing for the first time the beauty of the landscape through which we are passing. And reading for the first time the clues and the signals and the signposts around us, thus shaping our journey for ourselves instead of being carried haphazardly along like a leaf at the mercy of the wind.

How is this done? As is often the way with seemingly difficult questions, the solution is in fact very simple. So simple that we may misunderstand the meaning of simplicity, and think that simple is the same thing as easy. Such a mistake will lead us to undervalue the answer, and to try and put it into practice too glibly, only to abandon it when we discover that it isn't easy at all. Or, if we decide not to abandon it, we may then make a second mistake as disastrous as the first and assume that if it isn't easy it must therefore be hard. This second mistake leads us to attempt to apply the solution with grim determination, a determination that takes us ever further and further away from our intended path.

For the answer is meditation, and it is said that we should practise meditation as if it were a bird we are holding in our hands. Hold it too casually and the bird flies away. Hold it too tightly and the bird is smothered. Hold it neither casually nor tightly, and the bird rests between our palms and enchants us with its singing. In terms of our journey, what this means is that if we walk carelessly, taking no real heed of where we are, we lose our way; and if we walk doggedly, with our heads down instead of watching for the signposts, we lose our way just as surely, and often wander even further from the path.

MEDITATION

The next question of course is 'what is meditation?'. At first sight the word itself seems of little help. It comes from the Latin *meditari*, which simply means 'frequent'. Meditation is therefore something that is done frequently. The word tells us everything about how often we do it, yet nothing about what it is we actually do. It is like a ticket for our journey that tells us the times of our train, but not the platform or the station or even the town from which it leaves.

Yet the very imprecision of the word 'meditation' is in fact quite useful. Because it allows us right from the start some freedom of choice. It allows us to decide for ourselves which platform we want, and which station and which town. It allows us to set out on our journey without too many presuppositions and without too many expectations. It allows us to travel, yet does not dictate to us our starting point or our means of travelling or our ultimate goal. It allows us to travel, yet does not lay down a rigid itinerary. It allows us to travel, yet makes no false promises, gives us no empty guarantees, asks nothing of us except that we ask something of ourselves.

The result is that meditation is not a creed or a dogma. You may, if you listen to the followers of particular schools of meditation or particular spiritual or occult traditions, be told that theirs is the best way, and that if you embrace any other you are somehow getting it 'wrong'. You may be told by the followers of first this tradition and then that tradition that they have a monopoly of a truth denied to everyone else. Yet if you listen to the founders of these traditions rather than to the followers, you will find that usually they said no such thing. They taught a way, a path, but rarely denigrated other paths. And if you take the trouble (few do) of looking at each

5

THE ELEMENTS OF MEDITATION

of these paths you will find that in the distance, higher up the mountain, they seem to meet and become one, though where this one path goes afterwards you will have in the fullness of time to discover for yourself.

REASONS FOR MEDITATING

This 'open' quality of the term meditation means that before you start on the journey of meditation (or even if you are already well advanced on that journey) it is good to pause and consider your motivation for undertaking it. Perhaps you have heard that meditation can make you calmer, more peaceful, less anxious. Perhaps you have heard that it brings physical benefits, like a lowering of the blood pressure, or protection against heart disease and stress-related illnesses. Perhaps you have heard that it will bring blissful states of mind, or give you psychic powers, or make you happy, or even bring you to enlightenment (whatever you take the term to mean). Perhaps you have heard it will help you give up drugs, or deepen your powers of concentration, or develop your creativity, or improve your self-acceptance, or make you more loving and charitable towards others. Perhaps you have heard it will help keep you young, or help you live longer, or banish insomnia, or help in the control of pain. Perhaps you have heard it will make you more intelligent or more beautiful or more powerful or bring material success or make you wise.

Or perhaps you have heard none of these things, but are simply intrigued by pictures of yogis and yoginis, or of Buddhist monks and nuns sitting cross-legged and gazing with lowered eyelids into inner space, and wonder what it is they are seeing.

Look carefully at these motives, not because you must have them clear in your mind, nor because any one of them is right and all the others wrong, but simply so that, after noting them, you can allow yourself to put them gently to one side. Meditation may indeed bring you these things, some of them or all of them. But you will travel more surely if you begin your journey, your practice of meditation, with a mind that is open to experience, with a mind concerned less with a

6

destination than with the fact of travelling. With a mind that simply notes the landmarks as they pass by, that greets each one with attention, but then, without self-congratulation at having 'arrived', refuses to dwell on them and simply gets on with the journey.

With this attitude of mind, meditation is looked upon as a teacher rather than as a servant. For meditation, though it never dictates to you, will not allow you to dictate to it. If you embark on your journey with an imaginary travel ticket in your hands, your destination marked clearly and everything guaranteed – and with a return ticket as well so that you can come back if you don't like it when you get there – then not only will you fail to arrive where you want to be, you will risk failing even to leave your starting point.

DESCRIPTIONS OF MEDITATION

One of the best descriptions of meditation is the one used in certain of the Zen Buddhist traditions, namely 'just sitting'. Or, if you prefer a more extended description, also borrowed from one of the great Eastern traditions, 'sitting quietly doing nothing'. And while you sit (to complete the quotation), 'Spring comes, and the grass grows by itself'. Sitting quietly, doing nothing. If this suggests that meditation is the path of non-activity, of non-doing, then this is only partly true. Because although much (though by no means all, as we shall see in due course) of our meditation is done while we sit quietly, the benefits of meditation carry over into our everyday life, no matter how active, to such an extent that eventually they permeate it as sunlight permeates a room when we open the curtains.

Think of meditation therefore in terms of *process* rather than of *goal*. Think of it as something that allows you to see more clearly what is going on inside yourself, in your own mind, in your own emotions, in your own body. And think of it as a process which allows you also to see more clearly what is going on in the outside world, what is happening *out there* as well as what is happening *in here*. And which allows you, once it has helped you reach something that looks like a goal,

BOX 1
THE BENEFITS OF MEDITATION

I listed on pages 6–7 some of the reasons people have for meditating, and suggested that you should avoid viewing any one of these as a 'goal' towards which you are travelling. It is better to regard each one as an incidental benefit. . . and then continue with your practice.

But what do we know of these 'incidental benefits', and is our knowledge based on firm research findings and clinical reports, or simply on anecdotal evidence and the claims made by meditation teachers? The answer is that we do have a mounting body of research and of clinical reports, and in both cases the evidence points to a wide range of benefits which can follow from the regular practice of meditation. These include:

a decrease in
- tension and anxiety
- stress-related physical problems such as high blood pressure, palpitations and abnormal heart rhythms, insomnia, stuttering, and tension headaches
- drug addiction and drug dependence
- depression, irritability and other negative psychological states.

and an increase in
- feelings of peace, optimism, and self-worth
- creativity, efficiency, productivity and energy
- emotional release, spontaneity and contact with emotional life
- openness to the unconscious and to repressed memories, aspirations and so on
- independence, self-discipline and sense of identity.

In addition, there is evidence that meditation can improve powers of memory and concentration, can increase attention span, and can help the development of patience and equanimity. Some studies have also shown it can be useful in the management of chronic pain. Individuals report that their 'attitude towards their pain has changed', that the pain 'isn't so intrusive', and that they are able to switch their attention away from it more easily.

to see more clearly into the nature of that goal and to realize that, for all its value, it is not the end of the journey. Other goals lie beyond, and other goals beyond them too, so much so that you may conclude that the process *itself* is the goal, and be content in that realization until the process shows you that even that is not the whole of the truth.

This is a good point at which to try the following introductory exercise.

EXERCISE 1

Even if you have already done some meditation, this exercise is still of great value. For the moment, don't concern yourself with things like posture and breathing. These are important issues in meditation, and I shall be dealing with them fully in due course. But for now, concentrate simply on the one preliminary task I'm about to describe.

Sit comfortably, in a quiet place where you are unlikely to be disturbed. If you have a telephone, take it off the hook. Now close your eyes, and think quite simply about 'me'. Don't ask any direct questions about yourself. Don't try and dredge up memories or concepts about yourself, or try to judge or evaluate or describe yourself in any way. Just concentrate on being 'me' and on what 'me' is experiencing at this moment. Be aware of what 'me' is attending to, whether it be thoughts, emotions, bodily sensations, sounds, or whatever. In essence, what you are doing is being conscious of what it is to be 'me'. The 'me-ness of me' if you like. Don't try and hang on to any of the things 'me' is experiencing. Simply observe them, with as much detachment as you can.

Continue with this exercise for a few minutes (the actual length of time is unimportant) until you feel you have learnt from it, then open your eyes.

What was it you learnt? Don't worry if it is difficult to put it into words. Maybe it was simply the experience of being aware of yourself as a living being, with bodily sensations and with a stream of thoughts running through your head. Maybe it was a consciousness of how little control you actually have at this moment over your thoughts. Maybe it was a realization that thoughts seem to arise from some mysterious depth inside yourself, and that you have no idea where they come from and how they form. Maybe it was a recognition that, in the midst of all these thoughts and feelings and bodily sensations, it is very difficult to know where (and who and what) 'me' really is. Or maybe it was the revelation that life – and being alive – is a very odd business, one that normally we take completely for granted, but which in moments like this we recognize as unfathomably strange.

Or maybe it was something personal, and none of these things. No matter. The important point is that this exercise is the beginning of the journey inwards, a journey which takes us not to another country but to a place where we are and have always been, and helps us, as the poet T. S. Eliot puts it, 'to know it for the first time'.

THE KINGDOM OF THE MIND

Now that you have started your journey, you have made something of a commitment to yourself. By the act of running through Exercise 1 you have already 'become' a meditator. And you can repeat Exercise 1 several times over the course of the next few days before you go on to Exercise 2 in the next chapter. There are no set rules. If you listen to yourself, you will soon get an idea of the pace at which you should be travelling through each of the exercises this book contains. The only guideline is that there are no prizes for travelling quickly. Time means little in work of this kind. Rush ahead too eagerly, and you will soon find the need to go back and retrace some of your early steps. Travel at the right speed, and each step will take you, surely and steadily, to the next one. You still may find the need to retrace your steps from time to time. We never, in a way, outgrow the earlier exercises as we pass on to the later ones.

There is a sense in which all meditative practices, no matter how advanced, are simply the act, as in the exercise you have already attempted, of sitting down and seeing – and being – who you are. But if you travel at the right pace, then retracing your steps will be done not because your earlier steps were misplaced, but because by retracing them you will (in the paradoxical way in which things happen in meditation) actually be continuing your journey forward.

The paradox arises because when you retrace your steps you find the countryside around you has changed from when you first passed that way. Like revisiting scenes in dreams, nothing is quite as it was. The journey of meditation does not take place in a straight line nor at an even pace. We move in and out of experiences rather like a path winds its way up the wooded slopes of a mountain, sometimes almost losing itself, sometimes appearing to double back, sometimes rising steeply, sometimes gently and slowly.

In meditation you are travelling through the kingdom of your mind. We each of us live in a rich and beautiful kingdom, full of an enchanted beauty, but our tragedy is that we rarely stir out of the one small village. We live with only the haziest notion that outside our single village street there are roads stretching away into the distance, there are open fields, broad rivers, tall trees, secret places, snow-capped mountains, a magical landscape under a clear and welcoming sky.

You have now made your first move out into that country. There are two wise sayings from the East that will help you on your travels. Take them with you, and study them from time to time. They are both deceptively simple. The first bids you just to 'start and continue'. The second reminds you that 'a journey of a thousand miles begins with the first step'.

2 · FINDING THE TIME

DECISIONS ABOUT TIMING

In making a journey, we have to take decisions about timing, such as the best time for travelling and the period we want to spend on the road. This is as true for the journey of meditation as it is for any other, and decisions of this kind have an added value for us as we set out on that journey because they introduce the idea of discipline – a somewhat unwelcome word to many of us, but a necessary one nevertheless. In all but the most casual of journeys, we have to keep to a timetable if we are to travel successfully. Our train or our aeroplane doesn't wait on our convenience. We have to exercise some degree of firmness with ourselves, whether we like it or not, and keep to some kind of schedule.

In meditation, this means setting aside a period of time for daily practice. A short period each day is greatly preferable to a lengthy period once a week (or whenever we feel like it). Daily practice is desirable for most learning or performance tasks, whether we're tackling a foreign language, starting a keep-fit regime, or writing a book. Daily practice ensures that:

- the mind and body quickly get into the habit of carrying out the task concerned (routine has enormous psychological value)

12

- mind and body have less time to 'forget' the progress made
- family and friends come to realize that there is a set time each day when you don't want to be disturbed
- your commitment to yourself to practise – and to keep up your practice – is enhanced
- the idea of yourself as a meditator more rapidly becomes part of your identity

Not only is daily practice advisable, it is also best to set aside the same time of day in which to do it. This again helps to build up the idea of routine. In a short while you will find that when the time for daily meditation approaches, your mind turns of its own accord to the practice, and that if for some reason you are occupied and can't meditate at the appointed hour you will be conscious of something missing.

As to which time of day to set aside, you yourself are the best judge. Many people advocate first thing in the morning, while others last thing at night. Some even advocate midday. Early morning has its advantages, because the mind is (in theory!) clear at such a time, and the meditation gives in addition the feeling of getting the day off to a good start. On the other hand last thing at night helps to calm down the mind, and is beneficial for a good and uninterrupted night's sleep. Midday, when the sun is at its height and when your own metabolic rate may be at its peak, also has something to be said for it.

WHICH TIME IS BEST FOR YOU?

Before deciding on what is best for you, take into account domestic considerations (for example it may be hard to meditate first thing in the morning if you have to get yourself and others off to work, or hard to meditate last thing at night if a partner is demanding your presence in bed), and your own biological rhythms. Some people feel at their best in the mornings, bound out of bed full of life. Come nightfall however, they find it a major struggle to keep awake, let alone meditate. Other people, by contrast, find they never feel properly alert until after breakfast, while at night their minds are open and clear.

Take these points into consideration, and then make your decision. You can change it later if things don't work out. A degree of trial and error is often necessary. But be clear right at the outset that meditation is not about falling asleep. Nor is it about a mammoth struggle to keep awake. In meditation (see Box 2) the mind should be relaxed but alert, concentrated and focused, rather than woolly and sluggish. So try and pick a time when sleepiness isn't a major problem.

The evidence shows that something like three-quarters of meditators find they practise best in the morning, and around a quarter last thing at night, with a small percentage opting for midday. None of these groups is 'right' and the others 'wrong'. Particularly for people who lead busy professional lives and/or have pressing family commitments, the best time is simply the time you find best. And by the way, don't feel guilty because you're 'sitting quietly doing nothing', instead of rushing around doing the hundred and one jobs clamouring for your attention. Far from taking you from the world, meditation is a way of helping you to function more effectively within it. Time spent in meditation isn't time 'lost' or 'wasted'. If you like, look upon it as a recharging of your energies, an investment that will allow you to pay more attention to the other concerns of your life rather than less.

HOW MANY TIMES A DAY?

If meditation is this valuable, people sometimes ask whether they should aim for two sessions a day (morning and evening perhaps) rather than just one. Do double sessions bring double benefits? They may well do, but in meditation *never be over-ambitious*. Keep well within the bounds of what is practical for you. One short period of meditation a day which leaves you feeling you want to do more is far more beneficial than two longer periods which leave you feeling the whole business is becoming a bind. Never aim to be a meditation athlete. True, there are people who meditate regularly twice a day, for an hour each time (and of course monks and nuns do far more), but they have worked up to this kind of intensive practice over many months and even years. To begin with, settle for once a day, at a convenient time, and strike a bargain with yourself that you will try and keep this up regularly for a set period of time.

A month is a useful starter, but if this sounds daunting, a fortnight is enough to be going on with. Even a week will give you something of the 'feel' of meditation, and will in all probability inspire you to commit another week to it, and then another one. Soon your practice will have become so much a part of your life that you will be able to dispense with weekly targets of this kind. Meditation will become something you do, like taking a shower or walking the dog.

ACCOMMODATING YOUR MEDITATION

Another question often asked by beginners is, does it matter if you know in advance that you can't meditate every day? For example, you may be an evening meditator, and know that every Saturday night you come in late and full of the party spirit. Having missed your meditation time, you know you are unlikely to be able to motivate yourself to do anything about it, and in any case you will feel so tired that you will just fall asleep. So what do you do? Give up the meditation once a week, or give up your Saturday night out?

The answer is that meditation must have a secure place in the routine of your life, but security is not the same thing as inflexibility. In the early weeks and months of your meditation practice it's inadvisable to make too many changes in your life in order to accommodate your meditation. If you do, meditation is again likely to become something of a bind.

It's no surprise that many people, rushing headlong into meditation and enthusiastically extolling its virtues to all and sundry, are found shortly afterwards to have given it up altogether. Even the most adaptable and the most dedicated among us is only likely to be able to accommodate changes to the routine of our lives in relatively easy stages. Making a big effort right from the start to organize your whole life around your meditation is one of the surest ways of numbering yourself amongst those who drop the practice soon after starting.

So keep your Saturday night out. But – and it is an important but – try on Saturday to do a short meditation of a different kind at some other time during the day. A meditation that doesn't involve the formal act of sitting (see Chapter 3). This not only helps to keep your practice regular (we never expect a day off from living, and meditation is only the direct experience of being alive), but also gives you an opportunity to broaden your practice, so that one day you will be able to undertake it whenever you wish and wherever you are.

While we are on the subject of nights out, it's as well to stress that taking up meditation shouldn't take you from your friends. To begin with, they will probably regard you as a little odd (and until your practice is well established it's often better not to talk about it to others unless they ask first), and you may before long begin to make a new circle of friends from amongst other meditators. But your friends are your friends, and it is as ill advised to change them solely in order to meditate as it is drastically to change the routine of your life.

Certainly change is likely to come, firstly in the inner perspective with which you view life, and secondly in your response to daily living. But a useful overall guideline is to allow meditation (in its own way, in its own time, and only when you are ready for it) to change your life, rather than to change your life in order to meditate.

HOW LONG?

The next question is, how long should each meditation session last? Should you set yourself a target of ten minutes or fifteen minutes, of twenty or thirty minutes a day? Or even more? And how, if you are deep in meditation, do you know that your time is up? Should you set an alarm? Or ask someone else to come and tell you? Or is there a way in which your body will let you know that the allotted period is over?

The best advice for beginners is not to be too conscious of time. Keep in mind the idea of five minutes or so, and when

BOX 2
WHAT MEDITATION ISN'T – AND IS

I mentioned earlier that meditation isn't about falling asleep. This brings me to the many misconceptions that exist about meditation, and the question often asked by beginners (and by experienced meditators too sometimes!): 'How do I know I'm meditating?'. Let's set out some of the things meditation is and isn't, starting with the latter.

Meditation isn't:
- falling asleep
- going into a trance
- shutting yourself off from reality and becoming unworldly
- being selfish
- doing something 'unnatural'
- becoming lost in thought
- forgetting where you are

Meditation is:
- keeping the mind alert and attentive
- keeping the mind focused and concentrated
- becoming more aware of the world
- becoming more human
- knowing where you are

I am frequently asked if meditation is like hypnosis. The two could hardly be more different. Hypnosis is a drowsy, almost drugged state, whereas meditation is a state of heightened consciousness. Both states can be described as pleasant, but there the similarity between them ends.

I'm also asked whether meditation is an 'altered state of consciousness'. In a sense, yes it is, although it would be more accurate to describe it as a rediscovery of one's 'normal' state of consciousness, the state of awareness in which we would always be functioning had it not become overlaid by the 101 distractions we habitually allow to dominate each moment of our waking lives.

If your mind is really in the alert yet relaxed state which characterizes meditation, you will find that even if you feel sleepy when you begin your practice, the sleepiness soon passes. And there is some medical evidence that meditation rests and restores both body and mind more fully even than sleep itself.

the time is up you will automatically feel it's right to stop. It doesn't matter in the least if you go over or under the five minutes at first. After a few days, you will find your mind tunes in to this period of time, and knows of itself when it's over. Don't be tempted to go on much longer than this, however successful your meditation seems to be. A gradual approach to the subtle business of meditation, particularly if you are working on your own without a teacher (see Chapter 7) is much better than a full-scale frontal assault.

After you have been practising meditation for some little time (it may be days, it may be weeks, depending upon you) you will find a strange thing happens. Your period of five minutes begins to lengthen of its own accord. It still feels like five minutes, but when you subsequently look at your watch you will find that little by little it stretches into ten minutes, then fifteen minutes and so on. For time does funny things in meditation. In fact, the mind seems to operate partly outside time altogether, so that you lose your sense of it. Finally, you will find yourself sitting for twenty minutes or half an hour each day, and this period will feel 'right' for you.

Naturally this won't happen if you keep a sense of urgency at the back of your mind. Perhaps you are meditating in the morning and have the nagging awareness that it's nearly time to start the schedule of the day. If this is your problem, either get up a little earlier, or switch to meditating at night.

Once you have reached the length of time that feels right for you, you can now start to discipline yourself by sitting for just that little bit longer. If twenty minutes feels right you can try sitting for twenty–five, or if thirty seems right you can try sitting for forty. Don't push yourself too hard. There are no prizes for sitting longer. But the extra time is a way of gently coaxing the mind into becoming that bit more disciplined, that bit more concentrated. But I cannot emphasize too strongly that meditation should never become a burden. There will be times enough, in all conscience, when you will feel like giving up (and it's important to bring yourself through these times – see Chapter 6), so the last thing you want to do is make things even harder.

If and when you do set yourself to sit a little longer than your normal period, you will need something to tell you when time is up. Set an alarm, but choose one with a sound that is soft and peaceful. This is better than distracting yourself in order to peep at your watch. It's also better than relying on someone else to tell you. But whichever method you adopt, it's very important to sit for the amount of time you intend. Not only does this help to create the necessary discipline, it is often in these 'difficult' last few minutes, when we feel like giving up, that we gain most insight into ourselves (see Chapter 5).

WHERE TO SIT

If meditation is to become a regular feature of your life, you need to respect both your own individuality and your need for discipline. As we've seen, this means finding your own rhythm in meditation, your own 'right' time of day and your own 'right' length for each session. And it also means finding your own 'right' place.

This is more important than you might think. Certainly you should be able to meditate anywhere, outdoors or indoors, and a time will come when you will be able to do so. But particularly in the early stages of your practice, a special place where you go each time to do your meditation is enormously helpful. It sets up, like a regular time of day, a number of associations which serve to turn your mind towards your practice, so much so that you may well feel a sense of being welcomed, as if the time and the place are waiting expectantly for you, ready to smile on you and share the meditative experience with you.

Some people describe this as setting up positive 'vibrations', and if this makes sense to you then by all means think of it in this way. But the idea of creating the right kind of associations is just as good. Your special place becomes linked in your thoughts and your emotions with the inner peace you experience in your meditation, and with the calmness and the sense of harmony and of everything being just as it should be that arise during the meditative experience itself. You may like to think of this special place as a place of power, where you become one with your surroundings and build up the energies you need to cope with life.

This place of power can be a corner of a bedroom or of a living room or, if you're lucky enough to have the space, a small room devoted just to the purpose. In summer, it can be a place in the garden, hidden from public view (though I know one young lady who meditates naked in her garden and blithely disregards the curiosity of her neighbours). It helps if you decorate this special place in some way – perhaps with pictures that have a special meaning for you, perhaps with a statue (rupa) of the Buddha, the prince of meditators. Or perhaps with a religious symbol such as the cross, or with a mandela or a yantra (see Chapter 6).

If circumstances rule this out, no matter. The important thing is that you are there. But you might like to consider constructing a small bench-like table, about half a metre by 15 centimetres (18 by 6 inches), and standing no more than 10 centimetres or so (4 inches) high. You can keep this with your meditation cushion (see Chapter 3), and place it in front of you to support your rupa or your cross each time you sit. You can also use it to support an incense burner, since the presence of incense is another association which will help create the idea in your mind of a place of power. Find which incense suits you best (sandalwood and jasmine are among my favourites), and burn a stick that will last roughly the length of your meditation. Set it far enough away so that you don't inhale the smoke directly. Of itself, the fragrance of incense has a calming effect, and over a period of time this fragrance will come to permeate your place of power, and the clothes you wear to meditate.

CLOTHES FOR MEDITATION

Does this mention of clothes mean that you have to wear something special? Again, this is a matter of finding what is best for you. You certainly need to be comfortable during meditation, so tight clothes should be avoided. And there's no reason why you shouldn't emulate the young lady I mentioned a moment ago and meditate naked if you wish. A special garment, whether it be a robe, a tracksuit, nightwear or your bare skin, provides you with another 'prop' which helps to turn your mind in the right direction. But if the idea of changing your clothes in order to meditate is too much of an effort, then dispense with it, at least until your practice is well established. The crucial thing is always the meditation itself, and you should avoid anything that might put you off doing it regularly.

In addition to wearing something comfortable, you also need to keep warm in meditation. Not so warm that you become hot, but warm enough so that cold is not a distraction. Once again, when your practice is well established, you will be able to meditate in near-freezing conditions without noticing it, but in the early stages don't subject yourself to extremes. Keep the temperature at a level that allows you to feel comfortable, whatever you happen to be wearing; avoid any draughts (particularly important if you are sitting on the floor), unplug the telephone or take it off the hook if there's no one else in the house to answer it, and put yourself into a space in which you feel at ease and in which no one is likely to disturb you.

Then, as we shall see in the next chapter, just begin. But before you do so, try this simple exercise.

EXERCISE 2

Since meditation involves the body as well as the mind, it is useful to do a little preliminary work on it. Sit quietly as in Exercise 1 (page 9), and become aware of being 'me' once more. Just 'me', sitting here with 'myself'. Sit as still as you can. Now become aware of bodily discomfort after a short while, and the urge to change position. Notice how habitual this urge has become. Even though the discomfort is probably very slight, there is the wish to deal with it by moving.

Allow yourself to move. Now watch for discomfort again, and the urge once more to move. This time, sit through the urge. Notice that it is perfectly possible to resist it. Don't sit with it until you reach the point where you have a bad pain, but do be aware of the restlessness of your mind, and of the way in which this restlessness is reflected in physical movement. As soon as the mind encounters anything it thinks it dislikes, it urges you to act in order to remove it. It is this urge and its attendant restlessness which sets up tensions. Gently allow yourself to sit through this urge. Stay still. Notice how stilling the body helps you to still the mind.

3 · MEDITATION POSITIONS

HOW TO SIT

Exercise 2 at the end of the last chapter helped you recognize that the human body isn't comfortable in any one position for any length of time. Yet in meditation it's important to sit in stillness. The mind cannot become calm and still if the body is constantly fidgeting about. Mind and body are closely linked, in ways that modern psychology is only just coming to recognize, and we know that in stilling the body we are helping to still the mind. Similarly, we know that when stilling the mind we automatically have a stilling effect upon the body.

But if you are to sit still, you have to find a position in which your body can minimize the discomfort that prompts it to shift uneasily every few minutes. The secret of such a position is balance. If the body is properly balanced, then it can learn, with a little practice, to remain as it is for anything up to and even beyond an hour at a time. And the body is constructed in such a way that, if we allow it, it balances itself. It is composed of two more or less equal sides, left and right, a spine running down the middle which supports itself rather like a stack of coins, and a neck and head which, though heavy in themselves, cause us no problems if they are balanced correctly over this stack of coins.

So in meditation, seek to allow the body to achieve its natural state of balance. The lotus position, familiar to most of us from pictures of yogis and of Buddhist monks and nuns sitting in meditation, is ideal for this. It provides the body with a firm base – the triangle formed by the buttocks and the crossed legs with knees touching the ground – and allows the spine, shoulders, neck and head to rest comfortably on this base. But unless you take up the lotus position in childhood, when you are at your most supple, you won't find it comes easily to you, even after weeks or months of patient practice. However, if you have your buttocks 10 centimetres (4 inches) or so higher than your crossed legs (hence the need for the kind of cushion I describe in a moment) you can bring your knees nearer the floor, and this throws the weight of the body forward, making it much easier to keep a straight (and therefore comfortable) back. This adaptation can be used for both the full lotus position and the two variants I discuss below.

Figure 1.   The Lotus Position

24

In the full lotus position, the legs are then crossed, the right foot placed on the left thigh and the left foot placed on the right. But herein lies the difficulty. No matter how hard you try, it soon becomes apparent to you that your version of the human body just wasn't intended by its maker to perform this particular contortion. The image that comes to mind as you struggle to get your legs to obey you is of trying to tie a knot in two stubborn planks of wood. It simply can't be done.

So you may prefer to settle for the half-lotus, in which one foot (right or left) is placed on the opposite thigh, while the other foot remains on the floor with the heel as close as possible to the perineum (the space between the genitals and anus). But since even the half-lotus isn't easy for most Westerners, the 'perfect' or 'magician's' posture, in which instead of being placed on the thigh the uppermost foot rests on the calf, is often best (see Figure 2). It has most of the benefits of the full lotus, looks and feels better balanced than the half-lotus, and comes to most people after a relatively short period of practice. Let's assume you decide to use it.

Figure 2.   The Perfect or Magician's Position

25

Figure 3.   The Modified Perfect Position

USING THE PERFECT OR MAGICIAN'S POSTURE

Proceed as follows. Make or buy a meditation cushion (a round or square one, 30 centimetres (1 foot) or so in diameter), hard enough to support you – and to keep you supported – the required 10 centimetres (4 inches) from the floor. If you can't find the right cushion, any firm object of the appropriate thickness will do to start with, though it's a good idea to obtain a cushion as soon as possible, and keep it exclusively as one of your meditation props. Now sit on the cushion, with your legs straight in front of you. Bend your left leg, take the foot in your hands and draw it up against the body so that the heel rests against the perineum. Now edge the buttocks forward a little on your cushion, so that the perineum rests almost on top of the heel. Then take the right leg and cross it over the left, bringing the foot up so that it rests on the calf or nestles into the groove between calf and thigh. Your knees should now be flat on the floor, and the whole body poised and at ease.

You can reverse the position of the legs if you like, so that the left is on top of the right (and indeed it's a good thing to be able to achieve the position with either leg uppermost, so that your two legs become equally supple), but remember always to draw the lower heel in as close to the body as possible, and then slide forward on your cushion until you are almost sitting on it.

At first, you will probably find that once you are in the required position it feels excruciatingly uncomfortable. Far from your body being poised and at ease, your upper foot protests vigorously at the idea of being lifted up on to the calf of the lower leg, and your knees stick awkwardly into the air instead of resting flat on the floor. Don't worry. *And don't try and force yourself into the position.* In meditation, everything comes to those who are patient. You can try edging a little further forward on your cushion, or raising the cushion another couple of centimetres, but the important thing is to remind yourself that each day the position will become easier. Before long, you will be able to hold it without difficulty. Even the stiffness in the upper foot when eventually you release it from its perch will pass.

Some meditation teachers, particularly those trained in the hatha yoga tradition, suggest you should push down gently on the knees with your hands in order to hasten the time when they will rest happily on the floor of their own accord. But a better suggestion is to relax the legs as fully as you can, and then allow the leg muscles to press the knees down, slightly yet consistently, throughout the meditation period. Before too long you will find you can obtain the correct position without much trouble.

If, in spite of everything, you still find it almost impossible to bring one foot up on to the opposite calf, keep it on the floor and, provided your knees are in the right position, simply draw it up close against the calf into the modified 'perfect' position (Figure 3). Or sit in the conventional cross-legged posture. But be warned. For the body to be comfortable, the knees *must* be lower than the buttocks. If they aren't, your weight is thrown backwards, and you're forced to compensate by leaning the upper body forward. The result is discomfort, backache, and a feeling that meditation, when all is said and done, just isn't what it's cracked up to be. Since the knees are high when you sit cross-legged, you'll need a cushion or support that will lift and keep your buttocks 20 centimetres (8 inches) or so off the floor if you want to use this position, this allows you to cross your legs comfortably at the ankles.

USING A MEDITATION STOOL

There are alternatives to the positions I've just described. One is to buy or make a meditation stool. The simplest stool is rather like the meditation table I described in the last chapter, a bench-type object with a seat 30 centimetres (1 foot) long by 15 centimetres (6 inches) wide, and resting on two stout supports which run from front to back, but which in this case allow the seat to slope forward. The best angle for this slope is to have the front edge of the seat three-quarters the height of the rear edge. Some experimentation is needed to find how high the stool itself needs to be, since long-legged people will want it higher than short, but the important thing is that your legs need to be tucked comfortably underneath it, so that you are in effect kneeling on the floor, yet with the buttocks supported by the stool instead of resting on the heels.

If you're unhappy with this position too, sit in a chair – provided it's upright and you can sit in it with the lower back straight. Not only is slouching bad for the back and highly uncomfortable after a short time, it also prompts the mind to slouch too, instead of remaining in the necessarily relaxed yet alert and poised state. Make sure the chair is a firm one, and that it is at a height that allows you to place your feet flat on the floor. But unless you have a disability which makes it difficult for you to sit on a cushion or on a meditation stool, it's better not to rely on a chair. The very act of getting into a special meditation position is another of the props that help settle your mind into the right state.

From time to time, you will hear people say that the lotus posture or one of its variants, due to the position of the legs and of the lower back, allows you to control the 'animal' energies in the lower part of the body, and direct them upwards. These energies, you may be told, are the physical and sexual energies associated with the basic energy centres (known in yoga philosophy as the chakras), and that by directing them to move up through the body we enable them to become increasingly subtle until they transform into the mental and spiritual energies which take us deeper into meditation.

Whether you accept or reject explanations of this kind depends upon your personal philosophy. To some people they make great sense, while to others they are impossibly mystical and far fetched. But whatever you think, this should make no difference to many of the results that you achieve; for there is no doubt that sitting in one of the postures adopted by meditators for centuries does powerfully influence your state of mind. You can experiment with different positions just to test this for yourself. For example, I find that when taking groups of beginners through the early stages of meditation those sitting in chairs, no matter how upright, are much more likely to nod off than those sitting on the floor. And this isn't just because they're more comfortable. Even those sitting on the floor with their backs against the wall stay alert more readily than those in chairs. Try it and see. But if you do find you want to use a chair, adopt the Egyptian posture, with feet flat on the floor, hands palm downwards on the thighs and lower back straight.

POSITIONING THE HANDS

The final aspect of posture is the hands. You may notice when looking at pictures of meditators that some have their hands palms downwards on their knees. Others have their palms upwards, perhaps with the thumbs and first fingers touching. Yet others have the hands resting in the lap with the fingers entwined in various different ways, known sometimes as 'mudras'. Each of these positions does carry a different meaning, and when one's meditation is more advanced it

29

BOX 3
MORE ABOUT POSTURE

It's a sad fact that our posture is at its best in the early years of life, and from then on progressively deteriorates. Watch a small baby, just old enough to sit up unsupported. Notice the straightness of the back. No curve. No suggestion of a slump. Notice the older child, especially the fully mobile child of seven or eight, running or walking. Note the erect carriage of the head, the suppleness of the spine, the free grace of the movement. Now look at the adolescent, and see the beginnings of adult decline. The hunched shoulders, the droop of the back, the head thrust forward, the shambling walk.

Now observe someone with low spirits, and see the sagging dejection of their body. Compare them with someone in high spirits, and note the buoyant posture of the latter. The close links between mind and body are especially noticeable in posture. If you feel dejected, notice the transformation in your feelings if you straighten up, and look ahead rather than down at the ground. Finally, observe how much easier it is to stay awake if you sit in an upright chair than if you slump down on a sofa.

Once you are conscious of these facts, it isn't hard to understand why posture is so important in meditation. Whether you subscribe to the view that energy in some mysterious fashion 'rises up' through the body when it is erect, or whether you prefer simply to think of mind and body as influencing each other, there's no doubt that meditation is much more possible if your body is in the right position.

One day, as an advanced meditator, you will be able to meditate lying flat on your back in bed if you wish. But until that time arrives, a straight back, and an upright though relaxed posture, are the rules of the day.

can be valuable to explore and make use of these differences. Basically their function is to help the mind concentrate upon a particular theme within one's meditation, and as such, like the other props used in meditation, they have great value.

But in the early part of your meditation journey, the important thing is to keep the hands relaxed and comfortable, so that they do not distract. They can either lie on the knees or in the lap, as you prefer. If you would nevertheless like to make use of a mudra, the most universal one is the 'O' shape, discussed in Chapter 6. This symbolizes the unity of all things. The unity of mind, body and soul within the individual, the unity of the individual with nature and with the outside world, the unity of each of us with our fellows. At a more subtle level, it symbolizes zero, the 'nothingness', the 'emptiness', the 'formlessness' which is the unity from which we all emerge at birth and into which we all return at death: the nothingness from which our energies and our thoughts arise in each moment of our lives, only to sink back and be replaced by others in a ceaseless procession: the constant circle of becoming, symbolized in Buddhism by the endlessly revolving wheel. As is discussed more fully in Chapter 6, this mudra thus stands for the mystery that underlies all things, the question at the heart of existence, the point at which time merges into timelessness, the finite into the infinite, the temporal into the eternal.

If your hands are lying palm upwards on your knees, form this circle by placing the thumb and forefinger of each hand lightly together. If your fingers are interlaced in your lap, place the two thumbs together and raise them slightly so that they enclose an open space above the fingers. Or separate the fingers and allow the palm of one hand to rest on top of the other, while again bringing the thumbs together and lifting them slightly to form this open space. If you adopt this latter position, you will find that different traditions give different guidance as to which hand should be uppermost. Some say that if you're right-handed, the left hand represents the hidden, inner side of you, and therefore should be on top, and vice versa if you're left-handed. Others say that the right hand should go on top, since it symbolizes your determination to remain focused and concentrated in your meditation. Yet others say that the hands should balance the legs, so that if the right leg is on top the left hand should be, and the other way around if the left leg is on top, while others say that the position of the hands should be in harmony with that of the legs.

Whenever you find a wide range of opinion in a subject like meditation, where clear proof is difficult to come by, the conclusion to draw is that each teaching may have value, albeit in its own special way. The different positions of the hands should be taken as symbolizing different intentions. In the examples given these intentions are clear, and the best advice for beginners is to find which seems best for you. Experiment a little at first, but once you have found what suits you, don't keep chopping and changing. It's better to be consistent, as this helps the mind to attain simplicity instead of confusion.

EXERCISE 3

Now that you have found the right posture for your meditation, your body will adapt to it more readily if you take up that posture at various times during the day when you're not actually meditating. Take up the posture while watching television for example, or while listening to music or the radio.

However, when carrying out this exercise, don't hold the position until it becomes a strain. If your muscles become stiff, you will have to stop practising for a few days until the stiffness wears off. Also, remember to stay relaxed while in the posture. If your legs seem especially reluctant to cross themselves in the way you want, this is probably because you are too tense. Relax into the posture, rather than fight yourself into it.

MEDITATION IN EVERYDAY LIFE

One final word. When meditation becomes an established part of your life, you need to be able to enter the state whenever you wish – travelling on a train, waiting for a bus, preparing to go into a meeting, sitting by a river, lying in bed, even walking down a busy street. Some of these forms of meditation are very similar to your usual sitting meditation practice. Others of them, such as walking meditation, involve a special kind of alertness to your surroundings (see Chapter 6). These practices should be carried out in addition to, rather than instead of, your usual daily practice. But they do show that meditation, although helped by it, should not depend upon any one special physical position. If you allow it to do so, then you are rather like one of those annoying musicians who can't play unless they've brought their music with them, or the person who can never be happy unless every little detail of life is arranged exactly as he or she wants it.

Meditation is something you carry with you in your mind, not something you acquire from the outside world. It is your own possession. It can't be otherwise, since it's simply the experience of who you are – now, in each moment. Be suspicious of meditation teachers who say that you can only meditate if you do it *their* way, in accordance with *their* dogma. Discipline is important in meditation certainly, and it's an equally grave mistake to take up the practice imagining that you know it all in advance. We meditate in order to know, not because we know. But although other people can help you depart on your journey, and ensure that you receive a good send-off, they can't do your travelling for you.

4 · THE WAYS AND MEANS

You have already started on your meditation journey. The decision to meditate is your first step, and the act of sitting down in the right place and in the right posture is the second. You're now ready to take the third step. Or (since you are sitting!) you may prefer the analogy of a train. Having boarded your train and found your seat you are now waiting for the moment when it pulls out of the station and enters the countryside that lies beyond.

Van de Wetering, a European with extensive experience of Japanese Zen, speaks of the meditation position as 'the free seat from which you can roar into space'. Perhaps the symbol is too violent. In meditation one doesn't 'roar'. And the space into which one moves is a space which one discovers was always there rather than a space one enters for the first time. But nevertheless, the analogy is helpful. The meditation seat is the launching pad, the take-off point from which one moves from one state of consciousness into another.

But that's looking ahead. For the moment, you have simply settled into your seat, and are waiting. Check your posture. Check that your lower back is straight, and that your head is erect. Now check the rest of your body. It should be relaxed,

34

without tension, using only enough physical and mental energy to keep you in this posture without slumping. Allow your awareness to sweep slowly and carefully through your body, starting with the feet and legs. Are they free of tension? If they are in the lotus position or in one of its variants, are they at ease? Tighten and relax the muscles once or twice to make sure. Even if your legs and feet feel uncomfortable, that is no reason for clenching the muscles. Relax into the discomfort, instead of fighting against it. Fighting against it will only make it worse. Now check the buttocks, and next the abdomen. Let go any stress that you feel there. Proceed upwards to the back, the chest, the arms and hands, the shoulders, the neck, and finally the jaw, the face and the temples.

Be aware of what is going on in your own body. Tension is simply the body gearing itself up for action, tension which, if the action is not performed, we all too often leave locked up in the muscles instead of releasing. Think of the spring which activates a jack-in-the-box. We close the lid of the box, compress the spring, then go away and forget about it. We leave the spring clenched and tight, deaf to its need to be released and allowed back into shape. As your awareness sweeps your body, keep in mind the idea of gently releasing this spring, and allowing the energy pent up within it to flow naturally back into the rest of the body.

ONE-POINTED ATTENTION

So now you are relaxed, sitting expectantly on your seat. What happens next? The answer is deceptively simple. You concentrate. Concentration is the still point at the centre of meditation. Whatever system you use, it revolves around this centre. Meditation is impossible without concentration. A deep inner concentration, unhurried, without anxiety, without tension. The quiet watchfulness with which someone observes a bird from close at hand, knowing that the slightest jerk, the slightest involuntary movement, will startle it into flight.

If you prefer, you can use the word 'attention' rather than concentration. 'Attention' conveys more of the lightness, the

35

relaxation with which one observes in meditation. There is nothing fierce about this observing. Certainly it is focused and clear, but these qualities are achieved by gentleness rather than by effort, by the simple decision to observe rather than by a dogged, teeth-gritting determination to do so. One attends because one is attending, not because one is striving to use attention as a means towards some distant goal that lurks out of sight over the horizon.

There is a revealing story about a young monk who comes to ask the Zen master Ikkyo for some wise words to help him live his life. Ikkyo answers him by writing down the single pictogram for 'attention'. The young monk is puzzled, and asks Ikkyo for something more. Ikkyo agrees and writes down 'attention', 'attention', 'attention'. The young monk is even more puzzled, and asks Ikkyo what does 'attention, attention, attention' mean? Ikkyo writes down 'attention, attention, attention means attention'.

So in meditation you attend. In that attention, the mind becomes centred instead of distracted by the various thoughts that arise moment by moment, the various sensations that present themselves in the body. The mind abides in one place, instead of chasing off madly after first this set of associations and then that. True, thoughts and sensations continue to arise, but if the mind abides in one place the meditator is able to observe them arising and then passing away, like clouds crossing the face of the sky, rather than allowing them to take over and dominate this observation.

Attention of this kind is in essence no different from ordinary attention, but it is attention used in a special kind of way. One helpful term for it is *one-pointed* attention. The mind remains focused on one thing, on one point, and refuses to be distracted from it. It refuses to turn aside and become lost in the thoughts and sensations that arise. It refuses to judge them, even to try with an effort of will to banish them. It just lets them be, rather as we let a river meander along its own pathways but without letting it carry us away. The mind remains simply in a state of *awareness*, a state of awareness in which it experiences itself rather than the thoughts that crowd into it.

THE MEANS OF TRANSPORT

But if you are to attend in this way, what should you be attending *to*? Or, to return to the idea of a journey, if you are to travel, what is to be your means of transport? Here meditation systems begin to show their divergence from each other. Because you can travel on – fix your awareness on – sound, vision, words, inner pictures, a candle flame, a string of meditation beads, on virtually anything on which the mind can settle and stay settled. Each of these has its virtues, and I have more to say about them in Chapter 6. But one of the most valuable ways of travelling is on the breath. And there are good reasons for this.

- The breath is always with you, the companion that walks with you throughout life.
- The breath is rhythmical and balanced – a steady coming and going – and this rhythm and balance helps collect and steady the mind.
- The breath is a symbol of the life-force. Yet at the same time it is invisible. Like the circle, it thus stands for the emptiness from which fullness arises and into which fullness returns, the mystery that underpins this business of being alive.
- The breath has about it that lightness, that subtlety so important in meditation. As you relax in meditation so the breath, like the mind, slows down, becomes calmer, softer, less perceptible, until finally it settles into the merest whisper.

So the breath is an ideal aid with which to travel. Even if you decide later to focus your attention on another object of meditation, your early training in watching your breath will be invaluable to you. It will prepare you for these other forms of meditation, and you will be able to transfer your attention effortlessly from it to them. In addition, you will find that in each meditation session, a few opening minutes spent watching the breath before you turn your attention elsewhere are ideal for putting the mind into the correct state.

USING THE BREATH

Having settled yourself into your meditation position and decided to focus on the breathing, how do you proceed? Let's go through it step by step.

Lower the eyelids   There are open-eye and closed-eye meditations, and there are meditations done with the eyes half shut. Each has its purpose (see Chapter 6). But for the method you are going to try, either close your eyes completely or bring them so nearly closed that you can only see a slit of light. Either way is acceptable, though you may find that keeping the eyes slightly open helps prevent you from feeling drowsy. But make sure your eyelids stay relaxed. There should be no effort, no tension involved in keeping them in this slightly open position.

Turn your attention to your breathing   At first, just be aware of it as a total sensation. Notice how the breath flows in and out effortlessly, almost as if you are being breathed rather than breathing. Notice how it feels cool as you breathe in, and warm as you breathe out. Notice how the body rises and falls with each in-breath and each out-breath. Now turn your attention more specifically to *where* the breath is going. Is it going into your upper chest? Your middle chest? Or is it flowing deep down into your abdomen? The last of these is the correct place. In meditation, you breathe deeply, but deep breathing does not mean taking enormous gulps of air. It means drawing the breath down into the body as deeply as possible, right down to the diaphragm, the biggest muscle in the body, and the one responsible for the breathing cycle. Practise this for a moment, but without making any effort to take in more air than usual. Natural, relaxed breathing is your aim.

Decide on a point of attention   Now decide where it feels natural to place your concentration during this awareness of your breathing. Is it at the nostrils, where you feel the sensation of the cool air flowing in and the warm air flowing out? Or is it at the abdomen, where you feel the gentle rise and fall of each breath? Both places are taught in different meditation systems. The nostrils have an advantage in that the sensation here is more subtle, and therefore requires closer attention. The nostrils are also the point at which air enters the body, so they are the point of contact between the life-force inside us and the life-force outside us. But the abdomen allows us to become more aware of our bodies, and as such helps us to feel more in contact with ourselves. Experiment with both points of concentration if you like, but having decided on one, keep to it. Above all, never be tempted to switch from one point to another during a meditation session. Decide where the attention is going to be focused at the beginning of the session, and keep it there.

Count the breaths Particularly in the early stages of your training in meditation, you are likely to find that your concentration needs further assistance. This can be achieved by not only focusing on your in-breaths and out-breaths but by counting them as well. To do this, count each out-breath, from one up to ten, and then go back to one and start again. If at any point the attention wanders and you lose count, go back to one each time. This counting can be dispensed with as the days and weeks go by and you find yourself able to meditate for fifteen minutes without losing the count, but be prepared to use it again during those inevitable times when your mind is particularly active and meditation becomes difficult to do.

Now begin. And watch what happens.

LAPSES OF ATTENTION

At first, even with the aid of counting your breaths, you may find that the mind soon wanders away. Thoughts arise, capture your attention, and before you realize what's happening your counting, your awareness of breathing, and the whole idea of meditation itself has faded from view. Don't worry. Don't be impatient. Don't be angry or disgusted or frustrated with yourself. These lapses of attention happen to us all. For thousands of years meditators have been experiencing exactly what you are experiencing. You may think that you are the world's worst at keeping your attention properly focused, but believe me you are not. We are each of us the world's worst. But the more annoyed we become about it, the harder things get. In a way it's like dealing with a crying baby. The more we allow ourselves to grow exasperated, the more agitated the baby becomes and the more he or she cries. By contrast, the more relaxed and soothing we are, the sooner the baby settles down into contentment.

Remember always that it is precisely *because* your mind is so scattered and out of control that you need to meditate. If your mind wasn't like this, your whole life would already be a meditation, and there would be no need to find a special time and place in which to sit and practise. One of the symbols for the mind in the East is a chattering monkey. Each moment of our waking lives this monkey clamours for us to listen to it, distracting us from what we're doing, muddling and confusing us, making us forget what happened even five minutes ago, taking our attention away from life instead of allowing us to get on with the business of living it. You rediscover this fact each time you sit in meditation. Welcome this rediscovery. It serves as a timely reminder that you are engaged on a journey we should all undertake if we value ourselves enough to want to find out who we are and make better use of our own humanity. And each time you make this discovery, bring your mind gently back to its point of focus. If it happens ten times, if it happens a hundred times the remedy is always the same. Gently but firmly return your concentration to your breathing. Don't follow the chain of associations with one thought leading to the next and the next which the mind finds so tempting.

DISCOVERING THE MIND

After a while, perhaps during this first meditation, perhaps during the second, perhaps during the 102nd, you will find that the mind enters a state of one-pointedness, a state in which your whole attention is focused upon your breathing and your counting. For a moment, thoughts fade into the

BOX 4
PROBLEM-SOLVING AND CREATIVITY IN MEDITATION

Once you begin to develop the ability to concentrate upon the breathing, is it possible to concentrate instead upon a *problem*, and allow the mind to come up with a solution? And if meditation is supposed to help creativity, how does this work? Does one ask for creative ideas to surface while the meditation is taking place?

PROBLEM-SOLVING   Many people certainly do find that meditation helps them solve problems. But this isn't done by focusing on the problem instead of upon the breathing. Most of us have had the experience of going to sleep with a problem at the back of our minds, and finding the solution there in the morning. What happens is that the unconscious mind (the part responsible for our dreams) goes on working during sleep and, freed from the interference of the conscious mind, is sometimes able to find the necessary solution.

Something not dissimilar can happen in meditation. Although it remains alert rather than falling asleep, the conscious mind quietens down, allowing more access to the unconscious. The unconscious mind is just as active in problem-solving while we are awake as it is while we are asleep. The difference is that while we're awake we're usually too busy to listen to it. In meditation, we begin to listen. We don't even have to tell it to work on the problem. It is already aware of the need. We put the problem on one side, and as we come out of the meditation, we may find the solution to it comes at the same time.

CREATIVITY   Creativity is also very dependent upon the unconscious. Before starting to write or paint (or whatever branch of creativity you follow) you will find it helpful to meditate for a few minutes (sitting at your desk; no need to go and find your cushion and have a formal meditation session). Sit upright, close your eyes, and focus on your breathing. Don't think about your work. Allow the mind to open out and become clear. Then open your eyes and get on with the job. Notice how ideas now come to you more readily.

Sometimes solutions to problems (and creative ideas) come to you actually during the meditation, and there is a fear that these insights will be lost unless you get up straight away and write them down. Don't worry. Note them in passing, just like any other thoughts, but mentally tab them to be recalled after the meditation is over. With a little practice, you will find that they come back readily enough.

background and may even cease to arise altogether. The mind is simply there, doing nothing and being nothing other than itself. This is your first moment of discovery that you, the real you, the essential you, exists separately from your thoughts. You are not your thoughts. The strange dictum of Descartes, 'I think therefore I am', the dictum upon which so much of our Western ideas of who and what we are seem based, is seen in that moment to be absurdly false. It should be rephrased, turned around until it reads, 'I am, therefore I think'. 'I am, therefore I think.' Of course. How simple!

You won't put this into words at the time. The significance of this moment, when thoughts cease but yet you continue to exist, will only strike you when the moment is lost, for the simple reason that the act of realizing this significance is itself a thought. In that thought you lose this 'content-less' mind that you have just been experiencing. Even the realization that you have stopped thinking is a thought, and in that thought the floodgates to other thoughts are opened, and the moment is gone.

When you reflect upon this after the meditation is over, you will make a second strange discovery. Namely that you can only experience this 'content-less' state as unity, not as duality. That is, you can't be in it and aware that you are in it at the same time. You can't fracture your mind into two parts. You can only be whole, nothing less.

This and the various other insights that come to you in meditation are there when you are not looking directly at them, and gone the moment you are. They do not allow the existence of subject and object, a subject that looks and an object that is looked at. There is no separation between you and your awareness. There is no separation between what is being done and the person doing it. And therefore (though this may be difficult to understand until you have experienced it) there is nothing being done and nobody doing it. There is only a moment of completeness.

One of the best known of all koans, those strange riddles used in Zen which appear to admit of no solution and which push the mind to the limits of rational thought and then force it to go beyond, emphasizes this completeness by asking 'What is the sound of one hand clapping?'. How absurd. Clapping by definition is the act of two hands, of bringing the separate surfaces of two separate and distinct hands sharply together. So how can one hand clap? How indeed. And yet in meditation one hand claps. Or does it? Since no one can resolve the seeming paradox of a koan for someone else, this becomes the question upon which the meditator concentrates. And as we shall see in Chapter 6, where Koan meditation is fully discussed, it is the strength of his or her concentration and not the power of the intellect that determines progress.

THE PROBLEM WITH WORDS

But these are, of course, just words. And invaluable as words are, there is a danger that they can get in the way. So when I start talking about 'unity' and 'duality' and 'no separation, nothing being done and nobody doing it' I may on the one hand be confusing you and on the other setting up a 'goal' which you now feel you should try and reach. Often individuals, when they are beginning the practice of meditation, ask if they are doing it 'right'. I implied in Chapter 1 that the journey of meditation leads to an unknown destination, or rather to a destination that can only be known once one has arrived (when in fact the whole idea of 'destination' and of 'arriving' may change their meaning). So don't let me mislead you through words into thinking that I am describing a state which is 'right'. I am simply trying to put into words something that by its nature is wordless. There is a big difference, as poets tell us, between direct experience and our descriptions of that experience. That is why poets strive to convey the *essence* of this experience, the feeling of it, rather than to give a literal account of it.

A good example of this in poetry is the Japanese haiku, a short verse usually presented in English in just three or four lines (ideally of seventeen syllables in total), yet which encapsulates within us the sensation of having experienced what the poet experienced, of having identified at a level beyond words the 'nowness' of this experience, of having lived it through the poet as if he or she is recalling memories of our own past.

Take for example a haiku such as:

> Snow capped as they are,
> The gentle slopes of the mountains
> Fade into the hazy mist
> At twilight on a spring day.

Written nearly five centuries ago by Sogi as the first verse of a longer poem, these four simple lines speak to us as if it is we ourselves who stand watching the outlines of the mountains fade into the soft evening mist. For a timeless moment, we are Sogi and he is us. The boundaries between us have dissolved as the outlines of the mountains dissolve. With a few exquisite touches of his poet's brush, Sogi tells us all we need to know about the mountains and all we need to know about his feelings for them. Like all haiku poets, he identifies the qualities in an experience that prompted a reaction in him and gives them to us so that we can make of them what we will.

Take two linked haikus (in fact two of the very earliest examples that warrant the name of haiku), written over a century earlier:

> I wonder how it is now
> In the ancient capital of Nara.
>
> Those time-honoured cherries
> That bloom in double flowers
> Must be in their autumnal tints.

Again we are inside the mind of the poet, wondering with him about a place, any place, which we have left long unvisited but which still speaks to our heart. With the poet, we see in our mind's eye something, some intensely personal thing, that captures for us the spirit of that place. And with the poet we feel the 'autumnal tints' of passing time, the leaves and flowers of our lives changing their colours and shedding their fragile beauty down the years.

In the same way, whatever words I use in this book to try and describe meditation are an effort to convey the essence rather than the actuality of experience. If they succeed, then you understand them at a wordless level. If they fail, do not make the mistake of seeing in them something that is not there.

The German philosopher and Zen student Eugene Herrigel gives us a glimpse into this when he recounts his experiences while studying archery under the Zen master Kenzo Awa. In the form in which Herrigel studied it, archery, like the other martial arts, is itself a form of meditation, a meticulous exercise in total relaxed concentration. In the course of his long, often frustrating but richly rewarding apprenticeship with Kenzo Awa, Herrigel learns that Zen archery consists in:

> . . . the archer aiming at himself yet not at himself, in hitting himself – yet not himself, and thus becoming simultaneously the aimer and the aim, the hitter and the hit. Or. . . to become in spite of himself an unmoved centre. Then comes the supreme and ultimate miracle; art becomes artless, shooting becomes not-shooting, a shooting without bow and arrow; the teacher becomes a pupil again, the Master a beginner, the end a beginning, and the beginning perfection.

When, in the early stages of your journey, you enter a moment when concentration becomes one-pointed, you may experience from the inside what Herrigel is saying. And when such a moment comes – and this is crucial – do not make the mistake of attaching importance to it. If you do, if you start judging it, not only do you lose it for that meditation session, you may lose it for many sessions to come.

What happens is that the mind, having decided that this experience is a 'good thing', now tries to take over and re-create it for you at will. It says in effect, 'Oh so *that's* it; that's what you're after. Okay, I can set that up for you. It's easy. Leave it to me'. But this is exactly what you mustn't do. Because the mind will now try *consciously, deliberately*, to produce this moment of one-pointed concentration for you. And the harder it tries, the more certain it is to fail.

The mind has fallen into the trap of thinking that it can 'will' this state. That the state can be grasped, possessed, taken over and enjoyed like a drug or like a ride on a roller-coaster. But this of course is impossible, because as long as there is a mind trying to achieve this state and a state waiting to be achieved, you cannot experience that wholeness, that unity, which is what the state – in the limited way in which we can describe it – actually is.

And there is another danger. Namely that having entered this state, however briefly, you may decide afterwards it was rather disappointing. How ordinary! You had been expecting deep mystical revelations, sensations of indescribable bliss, long moments where you entered the heart of the universe and witnessed its secrets. A fleeting experience of just being present in your own awarness isn't what you're after at all. If meditation is no more than that, well then, so much for meditation.

Wait. You are still only at the beginning of your journey. You are again, from a different angle, trying to judge and evaluate, to stand outside your own experience and give it marks out of ten. You should neither be excited nor disappointed by what you have seen. This is the state of mind that lies at the centre of all states of mind, but because you have received a whisper of it does not mean that you have listened to the whole story. To return to the metaphor of a journey, you have seen something from the train window, but you do not yet know what it is you have seen. A gap in the far mountains perhaps, gone the moment you glimpsed it. But what was it you saw, and what was it that lay beyond? Only time will tell. If 'tell' is the word for it.

All this may sound confusingly mystical. You may look back at the benefits listed in Box 1 (in Chapter 1) and ask what has happened to these. Talk of a 'content-less' mind and of unity and of Japanese haiku and Zen archery may be all very well, but what about the more down-to-earth benefits like increased patience and better sleep and lower blood pressure?

Many of these will happen in their own time. Don't be impatient for them. Allow them to arise almost incidentally. But consciously try to use in daily life some of the ability you are developing for concentration and self-awareness during your meditation sessions. When carrying out a task of some kind, when listening to someone talking to you, when reading, bring to bear some of the attention you use in meditation. Try and be there in the moment, just as you are there in the moment during meditation. Don't let your attention wander off.

If you have trouble sleeping, focus upon your breathing when you get to bed, but this time with the idea not of staying alert as in meditation but of sinking down into sleep with each breath. It's the busy chatter of the mind that is usually responsible for keeping us awake. By focusing the attention on the breathing instead of on thoughts, the mind is free to do what nature intends and drift into slumber.

Finally, keep a meditator's diary. Don't be slavish about it. Write brief entries giving *descriptions* of your meditation, not evaluations. ('Mind particularly active; kept returning to thoughts of busy day ahead tomorrow', rather than 'Bad meditation; mind just wouldn't stop chattering'.) Note as well any changes in your own behaviour apparent during everyday life. Extra patience with a trying colleague for example. New-found calmness in crisis. More optimism and feelings of happiness. Don't go looking for progress. Simply note it as it occurs. Be prepared for it to fluctuate. Apparently excellent one day, apparently back where you started from the next. Note it, and go on with your practice.

If you wish, you could also record in your diary any particular insights that emerge during meditation or as an apparent consequence of it. But don't make too much of them. As on any journey, the scenery is changing all the time. Early insights may be supplanted by later ones, so regard each of them as merely temporary or provisional. Don't became too attached to them or they could get in the way of future progress.

5 · FOLLOWING THE PATH

THE VALUE OF PATIENCE

One of the most important possessions you have with you on your meditation journey is patience. The patience to sit. The patience not to become frustrated with yourself when your attention constantly strays from your breathing and wanders off after your thoughts. The patience not to expect too much too soon. The patience indeed not to 'expect' anything. One of the best descriptions of meditation is the one I quoted in the opening chapter, 'just sitting'. Just sitting and paying attention. Just sitting and watching, watching with the same absorption that a small child watches a much-loved toy. For the child, there is no separation between the 'I' that plays with the toy and the toy that is played with. In the act of playing, the toy is part of the child's identity, so intimately is it woven into his or her experience of the moment.

'But I don't have that kind of patience' you may be saying. 'I'm not the sort of person who can sit and wait for results. I like to get on with things, and I like to know where I'm going.' However, the very fact of your impatience is a sure sign of your need to meditate. Meditation develops patience, but patience of a very special kind. Not the passive patience that is often indistinguishable from inertia, but the patience that comes from the realization that impatience prompts us to skim across the surface of life, always seeking the next experience and the next experience and the next experience, and missing the quality of every one of them. Impatience prompts us to bolt the feast of life instead of savouring it.

In a way, you can say that the patience that develops with meditation ceases after a while to be patience at all. Instead, it is simply the awareness of the magic in each moment of life as it arises. Instead of patience, you could call it an absorbing interest. As I said in Chapter 3, don't set yourself extravagant targets of how long you are going to sit. Begin with only five minutes. If you feel your patience won't last this long, begin with four. We all of us start with *some* patience, however limited. Use what you have. Begin at the beginning. Don't ask the impossible of yourself. Begin – and let meditation help take you forward from there.

Exercise your patience in another way too. Many books on meditation present you with a rich array of meditation techniques. The temptation is to turn from one to another almost as quickly as you read about them. This only emphasizes once again our tendency to skim across the surface, rushing from one thing and then to another, and dropping each before it has been properly tasted. In the great meditation traditions of both the Eastern and Western worlds, pupils remained with the single technique given them by their teacher, often for years, until he or she felt it was time to give them another one. The problem in our modern world, where information is so freely available, is that we are metaphorically turning to the last page of our book before we have properly read and digested the earlier chapters. We want to know the ending before we have understood the beginning. We want to see if there are any pictures, any phrases, any words that catch our eyes. We want to know it all before we even know what it is we want to know.

So exercise patience by not trying to move too quickly from watching your breath to the other techniques described later in this book. Let me emphasize once again that *attention* is the key in all meditation, no matter what technique it is you are using. Attending to your breathing isn't the first lesson, from which we quickly graduate to higher things. It is the lesson that underlies all lessons, the first lesson and the last lesson, the 'essence' of all meditational practices, in the way that the haiku quoted in the last chapter is the essence of poetry.

THE BUDDHA AND MEDITATION

Many meditators in fact stay always with their breathing. It takes them to the limitless limits of meditation. They neither want nor need anything else. There is no sense in which they are less advanced practitioners than those who use other techniques. Listen for a moment to what the Buddha, who I earlier described as the prince of meditators, had to say when he taught meditation to his followers. After first advising the meditator to sit down (thus adopting a posture which is calm), to cross the legs (thus providing the body with a firm base), and to keep the body straight (thus avoiding cramps and aches) the Buddha goes on to say of him or her:

> Mindfully he breathes in, mindfully he breathes out. Breathing out a long breath he knows 'I breathe out a long breath'; breathing in a long breath he knows 'I breathe in a long breath'. Breathing out a short breath he knows 'I breathe out a short breath'; breathing in a short breath, he knows 'I breathe in a short breath'.

The Buddha goes on to describe the method of counting the breaths ('In counting he should not stop short at five, nor go beyond ten'), and to warn against following the breath on its pathway down through the body, instead of just watching it at the nostrils (to which later traditions have added, as I did in Chapter 4, 'or just watching it at the abdomen'). Notice that working with the breath was enough for the Buddha and for his listeners.

So even if you decide to use other meditation techniques such as I describe later (Chapter 6), keep mindfulness of breathing at the centre of your practice, something to which you return again and again, in between working with other practices. This strips away the complexities of some of the other practices, and returns you to the source. It grounds you in humility, reminding you always of the pure, bare attention without which your progress in any meditation technique becomes impossible.

STAGES ON THE JOURNEY

We now come to that point on the journey where we are able to see more of the countryside through which we are passing. Without becoming trapped in the words themselves, we are able to see that meditation involves essentially three stages which need to be taken one at a time and in a particular order. And yet, because this journey has its own rules, three stages which then exist side by side. We do not leave stage one when entering stage two, or leave stage two when we enter stage three. As you explore the three stages you will see that in reality they are one, and that although there are differences between them, paradoxically there are no differences at all.

The first stage is the one upon which you have already embarked, namely the development of concentration, of one-pointed attention. The next two stages are:

- tranquillity
- insight

Until we have achieved concentration we cannot achieve tranquillity, and until we have achieved tranquillity we cannot achieve insight. And yet insight is really only insight into tranquillity, while tranquillity is only the calm state in which insight appears. Two views through the same window, two windows through which to see the same view. And neither of them can be achieved without concentration, since tranquillity and insight are what happen when the mind is totally absorbed in concentration.

EXERCISE 5

You can of course help yourself develop concentration by practising one or two other simple exercises which can be done during normal daily life. Here are some examples.

Listen more carefully when other people talk. Instead of

allowing the mind to busy itself with ideas on what you yourself are going to say next, actually focus upon listening. Really *hear* what the other person is saying. And don't be distracted by random thoughts about him or her. Keep the attention focused upon the words and their meaning.

Take an object (for example, an ornament, a flower, a picture) and really study it for a few minutes. Don't become distracted by thoughts *about* it or by reactions *to* it. Don't label your impressions. Just look at the object. Allow the eyes to move slowly over it, studying it from every angle. Experience it, don't think about it.

Run your hand over an uneven surface. The clothes you are wearing provide as good a surface as any. Concentrate on the feel of the material, the varying textures of wool and cotton, the roughness and the smoothness, the raised contours of creases and pleats. Don't label the sensation, just experience it. Listen to the variations in the sound made by your hand as it moves over the material. Don't think what the sounds are 'like'. Hear them as they are.

I return in Chapter 6 to the question of concentrating more upon the things around you instead of being lost in thought, but try to use your developing concentration more in ordinary life. Begin really to look at and to hear the world, instead of passing it by, lost in inner preoccupations.

TRANQUILLITY

Now let us turn to tranquillity. What exactly does the term mean? Take the image of a pond, and imagine stirring up the muddy bottom with a stick. Watch as the mud rises, clouding the water so that you can no longer see into the depths. Now put the stick to one side and watch as the mud settles. Watch the water, little by little, becoming clear again, until you can once more see into its centre. Notice how still the water becomes. Nothing moves. Nothing clouds the clarity, so transparent that you can't even be sure there is water there until you reach down and bathe your fingers in it.

This crystal clarity is a good metaphor for tranquillity. Sometimes called 'calm abiding' by the meditator, tranquillity is that state of mind in which nothing stirs up the mud of our restless thoughts or emotions. Yet don't misread the metaphor. There is nothing passive, nothing stagnant about tranquillity. To understand this, imagine the water overflowing at one end of the pond. Imagine it overflowing gently, imperceptibly, yet once it has done so gathering pace and tumbling and cascading down the mountainside, sparkling and dancing and catching the light of the sun in a rainbow of colours. Yet in spite of its movement it retains that very same clarity we saw when it was part of the stillness of the pond. We can see without hindrance the bed over which it rushes, we can see each pebble, each rock. We can see to its depths just as we saw to its depths in the stillness of the pond. And we can watch how it flows round and over each obstacle in its path, arranging itself always with the same shining beauty.

It is the clarity which is tranquillity, not the stillness or the movement. Having its base in stillness this clarity flows out into movement, and if we look back up the mountainside to the pool we can see it retains its stillness. The stillness and the movement are descriptions of what clarity does, not the essence of what it is.

When you sit in meditation your mind, like the stillness, allows the agitations of thoughts and emotions to settle down, thus allowing clarity to appear. Or rather allowing clarity to re-appear, since clarity is always there as potential, just as clarity is always there as potential in water, no matter how muddy. And once this clarity appears, you are able to see that it exists in both stillness and movement, in the stillness of the mind and in the movement of the mind as it takes part, moment by moment, breath by breath, in the ceaseless flow of life.

Without this clarity, insight is impossible. How can you see into the heart of things unless there is clarity through which to look? How can you see the bottom of a pond if the water is muddy? How can you see what water is, if all you are looking at is the mud it holds in suspension? Some people ask if tranquillity is the same thing as relaxation. Of course it is, in the sense that when you are tranquil you are relaxed. But relaxation is not necessarily tranquillity. We can be relaxed while the mind is going through a peaceful daydream, or while it is recalling the pleasant memories of last summer, or while it is drifting in and out of a light sleep. All these states are joyful experiences, and of great value in and of themselves. But they are not states of clarity. Our peaceful thoughts are still thoughts, and we are still pursuing them instead of holding the mind in the stillness of its own being. Pursuing them is perfectly all right *provided we know what it is we are doing.* But if we mistake this pursuit for the tranquillity of meditation we are never going to see to the bottom of our pond.

ACHIEVING TRANQUILLITY

Does the simple act of watching the breath automatically put us into this state of tranquillity? Certainly, if we are able to just watch the breath. But for most of us the one-pointedness of watching the breath is a new experience for the mind. The mind isn't used to it. It is used to chasing its own thoughts, like a wayward child. It is used to setting up its monkey-like chatter, and dominating our lives from morning till night. So once you start sitting in meditation and watching your breath, your mind will do all it can to distract you. It will see this one-pointedness, this bare attention as a threat to its sovereignty. It will metaphorically tug at your sleeve with first one thought and then another. It will try and beguile you with happy thoughts, unsettle you with sad ones, distract you with anxious ones, remind you of all the things you have to do or should be doing, and – it all else fails – it will throw in a few erotic thoughts like a gambler playing trump cards.

And it will call up emotions to help. It will bring back the emotion you felt earlier in the day when someone was unpleasant to you, or the emotion you felt when someone was kind. It will remind you of the warm feelings you had when you did a good turn for someone. It will conjure up pictures, visions, scenes sometimes from actual experience and sometimes from fantasy. It will show you snow-capped mountains, dark forests, winding pathways, the strangely carved roofs of houses, castles glimpsed through the mist, the sea open and shining under a sunlit sky. It will make

these visions so entrancing that you may well mistake them
for the scenery of your journey, and imagine that these are the
places you have come to see. It will add in snatches of music,
the oddly touching words of a popular song or the crashing
majesty of a Beethoven symphony.

And if none of these things enable it to recapture your
attention, it will give you creative insights, solutions to
problems that have long been puzzling you, as we saw in
Box 4 (Chapter 4). If you are a writer it will give you ideas
for your book or your poem. If you are a painter it will suggest
pictures to you, if you are a musician it will hum new tunes.
It will urge you to get up and put these things on paper before
they fade. It will mislead you into thinking that at the end of
meditation, as sure as snowflakes on a spring day, they will
have vanished without trace.

The mind is indeed often at its most creative in meditation,
but for the present you are meditating, and each of these
distractions must simply be observed as it arises and then
passes away. As I said in Box 4, mentally tab any insights
worth remembering, and they will come back to you once the
meditation is over.

THE VALUE OF THINKING

Simply because they interfere with meditation, don't get the
impression that any of the distractions I've just mentioned are
necessarily bad in themselves. Thoughts, emotions, feelings,
memories, ideas are all vital to us, in spite of the fact that in
meditation we refer to them as muddying the water. Even the
inner dialogue that I've referred to as a chattering monkey is
often an essential part of life. We need to debate internally
with ourselves, to weigh up problems, to work out what we are
going to do and say, to go over past experiences and see what
we can learn from them, to divert ourselves with humorous
reminiscences, to use the imagination as a powerful tool for
helping us conceptualize and shape the future. We would be
less than human if we didn't satisfy this need. And we would
be failing to make proper use of that excellent tool, the thinking
mind.

Thought is one of the great gifts of the human race. Thought is part of our birthright, an inner magic whose true power is for the most part still only dimly grasped and used. And it is precisely *because* this power is only dimly grasped and used that meditation is such an aid to thought. Meditation is not the negation of thought, but its friend and companion. Meditation shows us that it is not thought that is at fault, but the *uncontrolled nature of thinking*. We have allowed thought to become chaotic, to dominate rather than to serve. Meditation helps us redress the balance, to make better use of our thinking, to allow it to become part of our clarity instead of churning it into a muddy suspension that obscures clarity.

The tranquillity experienced in meditation – and you will observe this happening relatively early in your practice – will begin to spread into your daily life. And as it does so you will find that the mind becomes less cluttered, that you are able to think more quickly and more clearly, that you will be in a position to weigh issues more objectively, examine arguments more thoroughly, see through problems more readily. Meditation will not help you become an Einstein (though it will help you realize you are someone of equal worth), but it will help you use thought more productively and creatively, and make your thoughts more integrated with you. At present your thoughts seem to exist independently of you. They arise at will from some mysterious depth within you. Meditation puts you into a position where you are better able to own your thoughts, as if they and you are on the same side instead of being constantly at odds with each other like unruly children.

Now let's look at the third stage in the meditation journey: insight.

INSIGHT

As I said earlier, tranquillity and insight are part of each other. They're rather like your two feet. In walking, although your weight is first on one foot and then on the other, the act of walking depends so much upon both feet that they form a unity. Without this unity, walking would be impossible. Neither foot is more important than the other, neither foot functionally separate from the other.

But if tranquillity is the calm abiding that allows clarity, what is insight? Again, the term is familiar enough to us. Insight means seeing in a special way into the true nature of something. But the true nature of what? In meditation, what is it into which we see?

The answer is, we see into the nature of ourselves. We see who we are, the reality of our own being. Not (unless we are very fortunate) in one blinding flash of revelation, but little by little, like seeing first one part of a picture, then another, then another, and adding further pieces until in the end we have the whole picture. Or to take the analogy of our journey again, like seeing one part of a country then another and then another until we develop 'knowledge' of it all.

I put 'knowledge' in inverted commas for good reason. Many meditators warn that in meditation you come not upon a knowing but upon a 'not knowing', an insight into the mystery of existence which is *experienced* rather than *known*. They will warn in addition that the very idea of *knowledge* gets in the way, since it suggests to us a formula that can be grasped and written down and communicated directly to others. Many Zen masters, for example, insist on keeping what they call a 'don't know' mind, a mind which is open instead of a mind which wants to categorize and label things, like specimens in a museum. Categorize and label by all means if you wish, they will tell you, but you will end up knowing only your categories and labels, and not the things that are categorized and labelled. Once we think we 'know', we close our minds to further possibilities, instead of waiting to see what experience brings.

These warnings are important. So, when developing insight, look for a sense of awareness rather than for a knowledge of 'facts' which can be reduced to simple statements. Look for an awareness which has more of an 'ah yes I see' about it than an 'ah yes I know'.

But where does this awareness start? Having begun to work with concentration, and having developed something of tranquillity, how do we develop our insight? Is there a recognized place where we should begin? You can in fact begin at any one of a number of different points, but as you are already working with your breathing, let's stay with this.

Insight into Breathing

The quotation from the Buddha on page 50 contains the words 'Breathing out a long breath he knows "I breathe out a long breath"; breathing in a long breath he knows "I breathe in a long breath" ' and so on. What the Buddha was saying is not that these words should go through our heads as we breathe, but that we should have *insight into the nature of our breathing*. Breathing is so automatic for us that we are very rarely aware not only of what breath is, but even of how we are breathing. Are we breathing in and out a long or a short breath? Are we breathing evenly or unevenly, regularly or irregularly? Is our breathing relaxed or tense, smooth or rough, soft or harsh? Is there a long pause between the out-breath and the in-breath? Are we *enjoying* our breathing, grateful for it, or simply taking it for granted? Do we know what air feels like as we draw it into ourselves? Do we know what sensations we experience as we breathe? Does the out-breath differ in quality from the in-breath, and if so in what way? Does our body feel differently when our lungs are full from the way it feels when they are empty?

We are ignorant in so many ways of our breathing, the very process upon which life depends. If someone or something were to stop us from breathing, in a moment we would become aware that the ability to take our next breath is the most crucial and sweetest experience in the world. If someone or something were to stop us from breathing, in a moment we would be fighting desperately for our very existence. Ask a person who has nearly drowned how important breathing is, and then you will be in no doubt of the truth of what I am saying.

So in meditation, since you are concentrating on your breathing, examine it closely to answer some of the questions I posed just a moment ago. Don't attempt to give these answers in words, or to form concepts about them. Just meditate on them, and experience them simply and directly. Are your breaths long or short? Do they feel rough or smooth, harsh or soft, tense or relaxed? Become one with your breathing. Feel it from the inside, identify with it so that you and your breathing are not separate but are part of the one experience.

During this exercise, it is important not to struggle to change the pattern of your breathing. But once you have gained some insight into it, allow it to lose any strain or tension you may detect. We are so unaware of our breathing that we aren't conscious of the violence we do to it. We aren't conscious of the way we restrict its natural in-flow and out-flow, either by narrowing because of anxiety or effort the air passages through which it passes, or by interrupting its rhythm. In meditation you can be conscious that this is happening. Without allowing your point of focus to stray from the nostrils or the abdomen, allow your awareness gently to widen, until it registers how the rest of your body is responding to your breathing. Don't confuse this exercise with actually allowing your awareness to follow your breathing, like a pet dog following its master or mistress. Think more in terms of a bird soaring into the sky and, though still gazing at the same spot on the ground, taking in more and more of the surrounding countryside as its field of vision widens.

Work with this insight into your breathing until it becomes a natural and regular part of your meditation. At some point during this growing insight, you will find you are able to dispense with counting your breaths. But even though you can now leave counting behind, be ready to return to it on those occasions when your mind for any reason is so busy that you need once more the help it can give. When this happens, don't regard yourself as slipping back. Counting is something you carry with you on your journey, to make use of whenever the need arises. Don't see it as a piece of baggage which you leave behind as your journey progresses. There are plenty of things you are currently carrying that will become superfluous as you progress, but the elements of your meditation practice are not among them.

As your practice becomes more established you will notice that your breathing automatically becomes softer, gentler, more subtle, until at times it is almost imperceptible. Don't be tempted to interfere with this process or to tell yourself that you should be taking longer breaths. This new way of breathing is a sign that your bodily metabolism is responding beneficially to your meditation. As the metabolism becomes more efficient it requires less oxygen. Your body has its own wisdom, and adjusts these things for itself. You will find it helpful, however, to take several deep slow breaths as a preparation for meditation once you're settled on your cushion. Release any tensions you may be feeling along with the out-breaths. Don't take too many of these deep breaths though. Three or four are enough. Putting too much oxygen into the bloodstream can lead to feelings of light-headedness, one of the last things you want while in meditation.

Some meditation schools also teach the value of swaying the body slowly from left to right at this time, before allowing it to assume its upright posture. Experiment with this. If it helps you, use it. Sway three or four times to left and right, reducing the extent of the sway each time, until you finish in your upright meditation position. This can help the body to feel more settled and more ready to begin the process of insight.

Other Forms of Insight

Once you are able to keep focused on your breathing and develop insight into it for fifteen minutes at a time, you are ready to focus your insight on to other areas as well. Stay with the body at first. I indicated in Chapter 1 that you should not make the mistake of seeing meditation as in some way a negation of your humanity. It is not a flight into rarefied realms of the mind and spirit that leave out anything as mundane as the body. Your body is part of your reality, the temple of your mind and spirit. Chapter 1 listed some of the tangible benefits that come to the body through meditation. Don't underestimate their importance. And there are other benefits, less obvious but of equal value, which have to do with a sense of being more at home in your body, of befriending it, of seeing mind, body and spirit as in communion with each

BOX 5
VIPASSANA

Meditational systems go under a number of different names. But in essence they are all variations on the themes of *concentration*, *tranquillity* and *insight*. The practice I have described so far, in which the meditator's attention is drawn specifically to these three stages, is usually referred to by the Pali term 'vipassana'. To be precise, vipassana means 'insight', and therefore applies specifically to the third stage, while *sattipatana* refers to concentration and *samatha* refers to tranquillity. However in the West, only the term vipassana is in frequent use.

Let's recap briefly on the essentials of vipassana.

CONCENTRATION In concentration, the meditator practices *mindfulness*. The usually scattered elements of one's attention are drawn together and focused, clearly and calmly, upon a single stimulus, initially the breathing. Whenever the mind wanders, it is brought gently back to this point of focus. By degrees, as the mind becomes concentrated in this way, it calms down, and becomes tranquil.

TRANQUILLITY This tranquillity is not a sleepy or trance-like state, but instead a lucid and alert condition during which one's usual preoccupations, distractions and anxieties no longer dominate and trouble one's awareness. This leads to a state of clarity in which insight occurs.

INSIGHT Insight occurs at many different levels, but it involves initially a growing awareness of one's own existence, and of the fleeting and impermanent nature of emotions and thoughts. Eventually, it can result in an awareness of the still centre of one's own being, of who and what one ultimately is.

Vipassana meditation can be practised anywhere. You only have to bring your attention clearly and firmly to your breathing, and hold it there, to experience the beginnings of tranquillity and insight. It is important that you should be able to do this wherever you happen to be, but regular practice, at a definite time and place each day, is vital if you are to progress.

FOLLOWING THE PATH

other, as part of the same continuum. These benefits lead you to be more welcoming towards your body, to respect it and its genuine needs, to experience it in new, more balanced and more harmonious ways.

This sense of being more at home in your body arises naturally once your meditation practice becomes established, but it's greatly helped by the intentional development of insight about your physical self. It is the physical self that gets you out of bed in the morning, that stands you upright, that opens your eyes and experiences the miracle of seeing, that moves freely, that hears, touches, enjoys the sensations of water on the skin, that breathes the freshness of the air, looks out at the sky and the trees and the rain and the sunshine, and feels the life-force that uplifts and gladdens the spirit.

Develop insight into your physical self by 'feeling' your body both from the inside and along its boundaries with the outside world. There are two exercises for doing this, both of which you should practice. The first, as with the insight into breathing, is to allow your awareness to expand from its point of focus at the nostrils or the abdomen until it encompasses the whole body. You may not be able to do this all at once. At first, you may find your attention skips madly back and forth between your point of focus and the other parts of your body. Simply note this, in the same objective way you note everything else in meditation. It is an important discovery about the nature of your attention, and shows the need for more practice. Then take your attention back to your breathing and try again.

Don't attempt to go too fast. Allow your awareness to broaden until (if your original point of focus is the nostrils) you are aware, however tenuously, of your face. Later, try to take this awareness further down, to the neck, then to the chest, then to the abdomen. Try and feel the body both from the inside (the sense of being in the body) and from the outside (the sense of being in contact with whatever is outside the body).

As your awareness broadens, so the details held in that awareness may become less distinct, just as to the bird soaring into the sky the details on the ground become less sharp. Nevertheless you should find a kind of very light, very

63

subtle overall awareness developing, so that without quite knowing how it happens you have a feeling of wholeness, of an integrated unified body instead of a collection of physical parts somehow held together.

The second exercise for gaining insight into the body, which you may find easier, is to allow the awareness to sweep the body, slowly and in minute detail, again trying to feel from both the inside and from the outside. In this technique, you deliberately allow your attention to move from its point of focus at the nostrils or the abdomen and to travel around the surface of the body.

Start by shifting the awareness to the top of your head. The scalp is well supplied with blood and with nerve endings, and is thus a richly sensitive area. Become aware of your crown, or of any place on your scalp. Can you feel something there? A slight tingling perhaps? A less definable sensation just of 'being', which may be the sensation of the blood flowing?

If you can't feel anything, don't worry. Your nerves are potentially perfectly capable of registering these sensations. Notice, for example, how quickly they register anything unusual, even the lightest tickling by a feather. But they have become habituated to the normal sensations of the body, and no longer register them. This is right and proper. You wouldn't want to feel these sensations all the time. But increased awareness of your own body means that you become able to feel them when you want to feel them.

Now, whether you register sensations in the crown and the scalp or not, allow the awareness, with focused concentration, to travel around the rest of the body. Allow it to move down to the face. What can you feel there? Usually it's relatively easy to become aware of the sensation of the closed eyelids, of the lips pressing gently against each other, of the tongue behind the teeth. Now move down to the jaw and the neck, now the shoulders. What are the sensations there? Again can you feel the flow of blood, the sensation of the skin against the air or against your clothes? (Don't move any part of the body to exaggerate these sensations; try to feel them just as they are.)

Now move down the arms, now into the hands. Feel the hands resting against each other or on your knees. If they are resting against each other, which hand are you conscious of? Can you be conscious of them both at once? If so, can you feel them merged in a common sensation, as if there is no boundary between them? Now sweep the rest of the body: the back, the abdomen, the buttocks resting on your cushion, the genitals, the thighs, the legs and feet – touching each other if you have them crossed, or pressing against the ground if you are kneeling. Feel each part of the body in turn with your awareness, almost as if you were stroking it sensitively with the tips of yours fingers.

If you have any aches or pains or sensations of discomfort, investigate them with the same light touch. Don't label them as 'bad' or 'good', no matter how strong the urge to do so. Investigate them for what they are. What *is* this feeling, this sensation? Don't attempt to answer with words or definitions. Just be aware of the sensation, and allow your answer to be direct experience, nothing more, nothing less. Not only is this practice important in providing you with insight into the nature of sensation, it is also invaluable in exercising pain control.

Part of the reason we experience pain as so unpleasant is that we fight against it, we tense our muscles around it, we resist it with all our might, we label it with negative language that gives it even more power over us. Once you are able dispassionately to investigate pain, to relax into it, there can come an awareness that the pain is 'only that', an awareness which allows it to fall into a different perspective. This isn't to minimize the reality of pain or the suffering it can bring. It's to alter the relationship that one has with it, to see it as manageable instead of as in control, to see it as a message which, having been acknowledged by the mind, can now lose some of its insistent hold upon the attention.

You needn't carry out the above two insight exercises each time you meditate. Nor need you necessarily carry them out for the whole of a meditation session. You may decide to spend the first part of the session watching the breath and working with concentration and tranquillity, then move to the experience of insight, then back into concentration and tranquillity. (Eventually, all three things will tend to be happening at the same time anyway, and will merge into that unity to which I have already said they belong). But do evolve a definite programme for yourself which includes regular insight practice, because there is a trap here. Tranquillity can become so pleasant that it seems something of an effort to carry out insight practice. But if you allow yourself simply to remain in tranquillity, you are gaining only part of the psychological and spiritual benefits of meditation. And if you are not very careful, your tranquillity will lose the clarity that makes it what it is, and degenerate into a kind of cozy self-indulgence which is the very opposite of what you really want.

Insight Into Emotions

Having tasted a little of what insight means for the body, turn it now upon your emotions. The emotions, though triggered by the mind, are felt as sensations in the body, from where they send signals to the mind, which registers and labels them and sends further signals back to the body. Meditation helps you deal with emotions not by fighting them but by giving you insight into their real nature, by helping you see them as physical sensations, and as physical sensations ultimately susceptible to control by the mind, both at the point where the mind triggers them in the first place, and secondly at the point where the mind subsequently becomes aware of them and labels them.

Gaining insight into your emotions means investigating them much in the way in which you investigated other bodily sensations. It means looking closely at them, 'staring at them' as one of my own meditation teachers used to put it. And as one looks, as one stares, one sees that these emotions, these dreaded things like fear, anxiety, guilt, anger, have no real substance at all. They are simply transitory physical feelings which we have chosen to label in certain ways. And as we look at these feelings, so we can see that some of the ones our mind labels as separate and even opposed to each other are in fact remarkably similar. Fear and excitement, for example, produce identical butterflies in the stomach, identical dryness in the mouth, identical sweating in the palms. Thus an adult and a child both going for their first trip in an aeroplane may be experiencing the same physical reactions, but while the adult will label them as fear the child will label them as excitement. Similarly a sportsperson and a stranded railway passenger may feel the same thumping of the heart and the same urge to do something violent, but the former will label it as being 'psyched up' for competition while the latter will label it as outraged fury.

Once you begin to look into the real nature of your emotions (and negative emotions are the ones most of us want to work with in this way; few people feel ready for the more advanced practice of examining their positive emotions too!) you will find that they 'open out'. They become transparent, they dissolve – sometimes into laughter – and they lose something of the power which they seemed to have over you when you saw them as objective realities.

You will also find that your increased sensitivity means that in everyday life you now become aware of these emotions as they begin to arise, instead of only when they have taken control. This allows you to relax the physical tensions that accompany them, thus preventing them from gathering full force. The result is often a kind of switching-off process. The emotion starts to arise, you see it for what it is and allow it to subside.

More importantly still, this increased sensitivity will help you to identify what it is in the mind that triggers off the emotions. However much we may be deceived into thinking that emotions arise spontaneously, there is in fact something in the mind that prompts them. So if you watch closely, you may for example see that your anger is born of defensiveness, from the fear that someone is attacking your professional pride or your possessions or your sense of personal worth. Or you may see that your fear is triggered by the thought that something awful is going to happen, or your guilt by the thought you 'deserve' to be punished. These thoughts may be so fleeting, so habitual that normally you don't know they are there. It's only as your insight grows as a result of meditation that you're able to recognize and identify them. You can then decide whether the emotions are justified and should be acted on or whether you can see their absurdity, and discard them as part of the baggage you no longer need on your travels.

In addition you can work with emotions if and when they happen to arise during meditation itself (usually in response to memories or anticipations), or you can decide deliberately to arouse them, for example by recalling an upsetting event that happened recently. If you use the latter method, decide *before* the meditation starts that this is what you are going to do. (Once the meditation is under way, your mind should not be indulging in the activity which makes such decisions.) Tell yourself as you take up your meditation position that as soon as you have focused the mind you will look at the upsetting event that aroused your emotion.

Once the mind is focused and the event arises from the memory, you will often find that it fails to prompt the least feeling of upset. This is fine. It shows the depth of your tranquillity. And it will help you handle similar incidents in the future without experiencing upset either.

On the other hand, you may find your emotional upset arising along with the memory. This is fine too. It will help you see not only the nature of the upset but where it came from. Was it from your feeling of being unfairly treated? Of being victimized? Of being neglected or slighted or ridiculed? Trace it to its source and recognize this source for what it is. Don't judge it and start thinking how to handle things more effectively next time, or attempt to discard what you may now recognize as your own emotional over-reactions. Simply note the source. You can return to the subject after the meditation is over. If you find you get nowhere with it outside your meditation, resolve to devote a future meditation session to its examination, after which things will become clearer.

Insight into Thoughts

Moving from insight into the body to insight into the emotions to insight into thoughts is to follow an increasingly subtle path on your journey. While it is *relatively* easy to gain at least initial insight into the body, it is more difficult with the emotions and more difficult still with the thoughts. Perhaps 'difficult' is the wrong word, since it suggests the need for increasing effort. I should say instead that as you follow the increasing subtleties of this path you will need more practice. The actual process of gaining insight is the same at each point on the path.

When working with insight into thoughts, the way to proceed is to establish concentration and tranquillity as usual, then to switch your focus to your thoughts. Watch them arise and pass with the same calm, objective attention that you use when watching your breath. Don't become attached to any thought. Don't try and hold on to it. Let it arise and pass as if with its own energy. If a particular thought refuses to go, and insists on stopping centre stage, you can in imagination give it a metaphorical nudge, like freeing a twig that has become caught in a stream, or like sending a captured balloon on its journey. If a thought still refuses to move on, stare at it in the way you stared at your emotions. See it as having no independent existence, simply as a set of words or pictures that your mind has created out of nothing.

If necessary, you can help gain insight into your thoughts by labelling them, something of a paradox since in meditation generally we avoid labelling. In this practice you use your own choice of labels, but these should involve emotional terms like 'frightening', 'exciting', 'intimidating', 'challenging' and so on, and also terms like 'memory', 'planning ahead', 'regretting' and 'hoping'.

Insight is helped by this method as it allows you to see the patterns your thoughts habitually follow. Do you notice yourself caught up mainly in anxious thoughts for example? Do you find yourself full of regrets for the past or for your own actions? Do you find yourself thinking positively about yourself, about your life, about your relationships, or thinking negatively? Do you notice a pattern of resentful thoughts towards others, or of jealous thoughts, or of envious ones? Look at what is happening. What are you being taught about where you are on your journey?

Your pattern of thinking tells you a great deal about yourself. Observe this wisdom as it arises. Don't react to it, don't judge it. See it for what it is, an insight into your own nature. Don't try and plan during your meditation what you are going to do with this insight. Note it, and leave it until after the meditation before you start to explore what it is telling you, and what this means for your future action.

If you want to go deeper, you need to know what is generating these thoughts. So much of our lives is dominated by thinking but where do our thoughts actually come from? What lies beneath them? If they aren't produced by something other than ourselves, then what is it in us that sets them off?

This question leads us to many different levels. In an introductory book such as the present one it isn't possible to go very far into these levels, but many of the psychological benefits of meditation come from this exploration. What is it in you, for example, that prompts feelings of regret, that makes you cling to memories, that urges you to plan ahead, that energizes you with hope? What aspects of yourself are you looking at when you see the thoughts that give rise to these feelings coming into being?

The answers are particular to each one of us, and only make real sense when we discover them for ourselves. But these answers must not be sought in the way you seek answers to the usual questions of life. You should not seek them with a sense of effort, of examining a range of options and sifting them, of testing them until you find the ones that fit. You aren't engaged on an intellectual exercise – or at least, on an intellectual exercise in the way that we normally think of intellectual exercises. Usually when we use the intellect we think in terms of our rational and logical faculties. In the present exercise, think more in terms of your intuition, your creativity, and in terms of answers that must be felt rather than expressed. Think in terms sometimes of symbols and pictures, of impressions, of an inner awareness that emerges without going through the step-by-step linear process that answers usually demand. Think more in terms of revelation if you like. And see how the revelation stands up to the realities of life, and to the next session of meditation. Don't regard it as 'permanent'. There will be other, deeper revelations to come.

As you advance in meditation, you will find that thoughts begin to lose their ability to intrude into awareness. You may experience periods without thinking (perhaps seconds, perhaps minutes, perhaps many minutes), and during this time you may feel what can best be described as the 'energy' of unformed thoughts pressing against your awareness, but as if the energy involved is no longer strong enough to break through. When this happens, investigate this energy with a relaxed, watchful curiosity. What is it, what does it represent, where is it coming from?

Don't be disappointed if you appear to make no progress with this, and if your thoughts still seem to be mysterious to you. Answers in meditation often arise when we least expect them. In a way, this is something of what the great spiritual traditions mean when they talk of 'grace'. One sits in the stillness, with the mind as relaxed but at the same time as focused and as open as possible, and one sees what happens and how it happens.

And in the meantime, be aware of what an intriguing, captivating experience life is. See how odd it is, and yet how wonderful it is to be alive. How wonderful to be this person sitting here in this body and in the calmness of one's own being, watching the breath as it rises and falls, watching the mind as it generates emotions and thoughts and allows them to pass across the clear space of awareness. Feel what it is to be alive, what it is to be you, what it is to be given this gift of grace, this precious human existence, with all its rainbow colours, all its sunlight and shadows, all its lightness and its richness. Remind yourself often that the journey of meditation is a journey into yourself, a journey into the inner country, into the hidden cities of the mind. A journey of discovery as tremendous and as awe-inspiring as any journey of meditation is a journey into yourself, a journey into the outer world and into outer space. And yet a journey very simple, very direct, very tranquil. A journey just as it is, nothing more, nothing less. Nothing to be added, nothing to be taken away.

And as you travel, see who it is that travels.

6 · OTHER WAYS OF TRAVELLING

So far I have discussed using the breath as your focus for travelling, followed by the use of body and emotional awareness respectively, and finally by the use of your thoughts. It is now time to look at other ways of travelling.

But let me repeat the caution given in Chapter 5. Don't be tempted to try a range of different meditation techniques to see if they 'work', before you have intensively investigated any one of them. Don't be tempted to become a tourist instead of a traveller. If you do, inevitably you will end up disappointed. Far from 'working' for you, the techniques will simply confuse you. Like a tourist dashing madly from one site to another, you will quickly become muddled as to what you have seen and what you haven't, and quickly drained of the energy and motivation required to keep you going.

Read through the techniques summarized in the following pages, and resolve to work on them not when curiosity prompts you, but when the time is right. I will look first at techniques which link in most readily with the work you have already been doing on watching your breath. But with all the techniques covered, I will try and show relationships with the three key stages already explored, *concentration*, *tranquillity* and *insight*. When you do decide to work with them they will therefore appear as extra details on a map with which you are already familiar, rather than as paths into new and unfamiliar country.

TRAVELLING WITH COLOUR

This exercise, particularly for those who are adept at visualizing colours, is an alternative to counting as a way of helping keep the attention focused on the breath. Use counting first in order to establish your practice, and having done this substitute the colours of the rainbow for the first seven numbers. Visualize red as you enter meditation and breathe out your first breath, orange as you breathe out your second, yellow as you breathe out your third, and so on up to violet. For breaths eight, nine and ten visualize two colours each time, a primary colour with what artists call its complementary colour (i.e. the colour formed from a combination of the two other primary colours) in each case. Thus visualize red with green, yellow with violet and blue with orange. These combinations are harder to visualize than combinations involving a primary colour and one of its derivatives (e.g. blue with green), and are therefore more useful in keeping the mind in a state of alertness.

When carrying out this exercise, try not to think of the *name* of the colour or colours concerned as you visualize them. Focus on vision, not on labels or on concepts about vision.

In some books you will find elaborate meditations on colour which make far-reaching claims about the spiritual power that the colour 'rays' help develop within you. Such claims are very difficult to put to the test, and if you are interested in them you need ultimately to experiment with them yourself. But there is a danger that some of these meditations may not only confuse you but rob you of time which would be better devoted to developing your basic practice. The present meditation has the advantage of allowing you to use colour while at the same time not taking you away from the essential elements of this practice.

After working with these colours and getting the visualizations clearly established, you can work with just one colour for a whole meditation session if you like. This is your opportunity to note the effect each colour has upon your concentration and upon your tranquillity, and further develop your insight by observing if – and how – it influences your feelings both during and after the session. To work this way, concentrate on the breathing as usual, but have your chosen colour as a background to the breathing. Imagine yourself surrounded softly by the colour, as if your breath is coming to you through a tunnel formed by and through it. If at any time this practice becomes disturbing, discontinue the visualization and return simply to your breathing, saying to yourself 'The white light of my breathing banishes all colours, and surrounds me in peace'.

There is no doubt that, whether or not you believe colour can have an influence upon spiritual development, it certainly does have a profound effect upon our psychology. Colour can affect both our moods and our thoughts, and gaining insight into what colours mean for each of us individually is an important part of extending our self-understanding.

TRAVELLING WITH SOUND

Sound has similarly profound psychological effects upon us. We notice this especially with music. Some music soothes, some music energizes, and some music simply annoys. We also notice it in the sounds of everyday life. We enjoy the sound of water – waves on the beach, fountains playing, a stream rippling over pebbles, a waterfall crashing from the heights. We enjoy the sound of the wind in the trees, of birdsong, of the low rumble of distant thunder. We enjoy the sound of human voices, of a baby chuckling, of laughter. Other sounds, though nothing special in themselves, we enjoy through association. The chink of teacups, the cork popping from the wine bottle, applause, the lawnmower and the sounds of summer.

By contrast, we dislike harsh, sudden, invasive, discordant or cacophonous sounds. Such sounds are useful in that they teach us the value of silence, but whereas pleasant sounds can soothe or excite, unpleasant sounds grate upon the nerves and can produce anger, fear, frustration, and even highly disturbed and disorientated states of mind.

In the light of its undoubted power, sound not surprisingly can be used to great effect in meditation. Chanting, plain song and sacred music are all designed to put us into an altered state of consciousness, an altered state in which we can experience being caught up and taken out of our mundane way of experiencing ourselves. Put sound and meditation together, and the result can be very deep and far-reaching.

One way of using sound is to employ a mantra. Deriving from the Sanskrit root *man*, which means to think, mantras were originally used in the Hindu tradition as instruments for prompting religious thought. Often consisting of lines from the ancient Vedic sutras or hymns, they allowed the mind to ponder sacred truths until these truths 'revealed' themselves to the meditator and took on a deep inner meaning. However in more recent centuries, and particularly in Buddhist traditions, mantras have been used as much for the quality of the sounds they contain as for any meaning carried by the individual words.

In fact, since many of the most widely used mantras are in Sanskrit or Tibetan, they are often incomprehensible to the majority of those who use them, particularly Westerners. In some cases, Sanskrit and Tibetan scholars will tell you that they are in any case virtually untranslatable, or if translatable will leave you wondering what all the fuss is about.

For example, one of the most revered of all mantras, 'Om mani padme hum' (known as the mani or great mantra), can only be translated as 'Om to the thought (mani) in the lotus (padme)' – or more usually 'Hail to the jewel in the lotus'. The 'jewel' can be taken to mean one's own enlightened being, hidden deep in the 'lotus' of the heart, but this meaning is for the most part less important even to Sanskrit and Tibetan speakers than are the pure sounds of the mantra itself.

Some of the sounds used in a mantra – such as 'om' and 'hum' in the above example, and 'swaha' which occurs in many other mantras – do not in fact have any direct meaning. They are sound for the sake of sound, and I shall have more to say about this shortly.

When working with a mantra, the syllables are repeated rhythmically, either aloud or to oneself, over and over again. Sometimes this is done with the help of a mala, a string of 108 beads which is held in the right hand and worked slowly through the fingers, with each bead held briefly on each repetition. Whether or not a mala is used, the mantra is best combined with the breathing, with a repetition occurring on each in-breath and each out-breath, and with the intention encompassing both the sound and the breath.

Instead of consisting of phrases, some mantras involve just a single word, which can be repeated a number of times on each in-breath and each out-breath, or which can be used independently of the breathing. If you are saying the mantra silently to yourself rather than out loud, it is nevertheless useful to say it audibly a few times at the beginning of each meditation, gradually reducing the sound to a whisper until it is 'taken into the heart' and said under the breath. This helps to establish the sound in one's mind, and the practice can be repeated during the meditation itself if the attention is found to wander away from the repetitions.

The teaching in most traditions is that you should be given your mantra by your meditation teacher. This can happen (as in the Tibetan Buddhist system) when he or she initiates you into a practice associated with a particular buddha or bodhisattva, and gives you the mantra associated with this august being plus instructions on how to use it. Or it can happen (as in some Hindu systems) when the teacher chooses a mantra which is claimed to be particularly appropriate to you personally. Or it can happen (as in Christian meditative traditions) when you are taught the value of a particular short prayer, and instructed to repeat it a set number of times each day.

If you are working without a teacher, the choice of a mantra can present difficulties, but these are sometimes over-emphasized. It is said, for example, that as the effect of many of the mantras actually comes from the sound of the Sanskrit language in which they are expressed, they must be pronounced perfectly. But if one takes the great mantra 'Om mani padme hum', one finds it is pronounced by Tibetans as

'Um mani peme hung' with no apparent loss of efficacy!

Indeed, disagreements over the precise pronunciation of mantras call to mind the ancient Sufi story of the sternly orthodox Dervish teacher who, walking one day beside the riverbank, heard someone from a hermitage on one of the islands chanting a Dervish mantra. 'That is no good', thought the Dervish to himself, 'the fellow is mispronouncing it.' Whereupon he hired a boat, rowed out to the island, and informed the hermit that instead of chanting 'U ya hu' he should be chanting 'Ya hu'.

The hermit humbly thanked the Dervish, who then returned to his boat and set off back, feeling very pleased with himself for his kind deed. After all, it was taught that if the mantra was chanted correctly one could even walk on water, though he had never himself been fortunate enough to witness the feat.

The silence from the island assured the Dervish that the hermit was now digesting the lesson he had just been given. But a few moments later a faltering 'U ya hu' floating over the water revealed that the hermit was, in spite of himself, unable to shake off his old bad habits. The Dervish rested on his oars, and was reflecting on the frailty of his fellow men when a strange sight met his eyes. The hermit had now left his island and was walking over the water towards the rowing boat. 'I'm sorry to trouble you brother' he said hesitantly, 'but I have come to ask you once again to tell me the correct method of pronunciation, for I have difficulty in remembering it.'

The important thing is less the pronunciation of the mantra than the dedication one brings to one's practice of it. In fact any succession of rhythmical sounds, no matter how meaningless, will put the mind into a meditative consciousness if repeated often enough and with the necessary focused awareness. This can be equally true of sounds which do have meaning, since the repetition can often strip this meaning away, and leave one working with the pure sound alone. The poet Tennyson wrote of achieving profound states simply by repeating his own name over and over again to himself. After many repetitions, the name lost any sense of personal significance, and Tennyson's own sense of separate existence merged into that all-embracing awareness of unity which is the hallmark of mystical experience.

I first experienced this phenomenon myself by accident as a young boy. Walking to school one day I noticed the road sign to London, and for some reason began repeating 'London' to myself over and over again. I still remember the surprise I felt when I realized that such a familiar name lost its associations in the process, and became simply a sound, a sound which seemed, as I continued with the repetitions, to strip associations briefly away from language itself, leaving me with a strange yet pleasant feeling of being one with everything around me. As the objects surrounding me lost their linguistic labels, so they lost the concepts that went with these labels, and became without boundaries, merging and flowing into each other and I with and into them.

But to return to the choice of a mantra. If you do not have a meditation teacher who can select an appropriate mantra for you, you can take any sound that you find has a particular appeal. It can be a word such as 'peace', or a sentence such as 'peace is in and with me'. Or you can take the name of one of the great spiritual teachers. In the Christian tradition for example the Jesus prayer ('Lord Jesus Christ Son of God have mercy on me') has been widely used down the centuries by the various branches of the Orthodox Church, as has the Greek 'Kyrie eleison'. Or you can take the great mantra, 'Om mani padme hum', which is in a sense the possession of everyone, since it is a direct address to the in-dwelling spirit. It is usually chanted with a long 'om' and a long 'hum', while 'mani' and 'padme' are said as a single word. Thus the rhythm is rather like 'O-m manipadme h-u-m'. For those particularly interested in the 'correct' pronunciation, the 'a' in 'mani' is usually pronounced as in 'father', 'padme' is pronounced rather like 'pay-me', and the 'u' in 'hum' like the 'o' in 'woman'.

Another alternative is to use the sound 'om' (written more phonetically as 'aum') on its own. This sound has been claimed for thousands of years to be the 'universal' sound, the essence of all sounds, and as such to have a profound effect upon the mind. When using it on its own, you can obtain the full quality of the range of sounds it contains by beginning with a long 'a'

78

(pronounced like the 'a' in 'father') in the back of the throat, continuing with the 'u' (pronounced 'oo') in the middle of the mouth, and terminating with a 'm' sound at the front of the mouth behind closed lips. Each sound should resonate or vibrate.

These resonations and vibrations can be felt through the whole body by making the initial 'a' resonate in the belly, the middle 'oo' resonate and vibrate in the chest, and the final 'm' vibrate in the skull, at the point above and behind the eyes. The whole sound should occupy the complete out-breath, and after several audible repetitions of it you will find that your body feels invigorated and energized, yet at the same time relaxed and centred. All those who scoff at the value of sound should, whether they meditate or not, try this exercise themselves (preferably first thing in the morning) over a period of days, and be aware of the results.

TRAVELLING WITH PICTURES

The essence of meditation, as I have emphasized several times, is keeping the mind focused, in an alert and yet relaxed manner, upon a chosen stimulus. I have discussed the use of the breath and body as focal points, the use of emotions, of thoughts, of colours, and of sounds. A further stimulus is the use of pictures or of geometrical patterns or shapes, either observed directly or held in the mind as visualizations. Let's take those observed directly first.

Since you don't want to give the mind too much temptation to set off on its usual wool-gathering, it's better not to use representational pictures for this purpose, though Roman Catholics use images of the Virgin or of the sacred heart of Christ. Instead, use geometrical shapes and patterns. The 'simplest' of these is the circle, a shape which occurs over and over again in the symbolism of most of the great religious and esoteric traditions, from the Celtic cross of the Christians to the Buddhist wheel, from the graceful spinning movement of the Dervishes to the yin/yang symbol of the Taoists, from the Egyptian winged circle of Ra the sun god to the Islamic cupola or dome of heaven, from the sacred space of the American

BOX 6
DANGERS OF MEDITATION

Mention in the text of the way in which we can strip meaning away even from words as familiar as our own names raises the issue of whether or not there are any dangers in meditation. Can stripping the meaning away from our own names lead to a sense of depersonalization for example? Can any meditation practices lead us to lose touch with reality? Can we encounter in meditation levels of our own mind such as repressed memories or emotions that we find disturbing?

It would be wrong to suggest that dangers don't exist. Almost everything in life carries certain dangers. Books and films can upset and disturb us. Relationships can upset and disturb us. Even wholesome food can upset and disturb us. But the dangers of meditation are not great provided one travels at the right speed, and provided always that one remembers meditation is a way of gaining insight *into* reality rather than a way of escaping *from* reality. Let's look at one or two of these dangers in more detail.

DEPERSONALIZATION There's no doubt that, if we go into a trance-like state in meditation instead of keeping the mind alert and focused, we can experience when we emerge from it a sense of disorientation, of not knowing where we are, of losing touch with the world and with our own identity. This is not unlike the depersonalization we may experience if woken suddenly from a deep sleep. The lesson to be learnt is simple. Keep the mind always aware of what it is you're doing. If you're watching the breath, then watch the breath. If you are visualizing a colour, you are visualizing a colour, and so on.

Chanting, mantra meditation, and exercises such as repeating your own name over and over again are more likely to lead to depersonalization than watching the breath. If you find this is the case, stay with the breath. Your breath will always ground you, will always calm and reassure you. What else can it do? In a sense, it is your best friend.

EXTRA-SENSORY PERCEPTION Most of the great meditation traditions teach that meditators sometimes find themselves gaining powers of extra-sensory perception such as telepathy and clairvoyance at a certain stage in their practice. These powers are known in Sanskrit as *siddhis* and the teaching is that they can become a distraction, and that one should simply observe them (or use them occasionally when they are helpful to others), rather than employ them in the service of the self or see them as a source of pride.

Science has always been divided on the existence of extra-sensory perception. Some scientists regard it as proven virtually beyond doubt by carefully controlled experiments, others dismiss it as superstition and delusion. The only way to resolve the issue for oneself is through personal experience. When you start to meditate, you may find your dreams become more vivid, that you recall them more clearly upon waking, and that you even encounter lucid dreams (those dreams in which we are consciously aware we are dreaming) and out-of-the-body experiences. Sometimes information may come to you in these dreams which you feel is telepathic or clairvoyant. In waking life, you may have sudden flashes of intuition which you feel carry the same interpretation.

Note these things, and see what they appear to mean and to prove. But remember, they are incidental to, not the purpose of, your meditation practice.

Indians to the Prakriti circle of the Hindus. From the Laps to the Incas, from the Siberian shaman to the Kalahari bushpeople, the circle has been regarded as possessing sacred meaning.

As such, the circle is held to symbolize wholeness, totality, completion, perfection, fulfilment, the rhythm of life, the constant outgoing and returning of existence, the unity of all things, the absolute. If a dot is placed at its centre, this represents the still point in the middle, the eternal axis around which the world of forms revolves. The circle now symbolizes motion, change, yet at the same time the absence of change. The circle can spin on its axis, yet however fast it moves it still remains a circle, and each point on its circumference still remains an integral and equally valuable part of the whole.

The circle also symbolizes form and emptiness, emptiness and form. The circumference of the circle encloses empty space, yet the space inside and outside the circumference can be said to enclose the circumference. What, therefore, defines the circle? The circumference or the space, the form or the emptiness?

Because of these rich symbolic meanings, the circle therefore provides an ideal focus for meditation. But be clear how symbols like the circle work. They do not work through the meaning you *attach* to them. When meditating on a circle, you therefore don't concentrate upon the verbal interpretations of the symbol to which I've just referred (and the many more you can probably think of for yourself). A symbol such as the circle doesn't need words. It speaks directly to you, and only afterwards do you find the need to translate its language into words. Symbols such as the circle hold a power in and of themselves, a power which modern psychology recognizes without being able fully to explain. Certain symbols appear to be keys which put us into closer touch with the material of our own unconscious. They occur spontaneously in the language of the unconscious such as dreams, and by holding them in our minds we are able to experience their power to heal, to inform, to calm the mind, to broaden its boundaries and to take us into deeper and deeper levels of our own consciousness.

When meditating on the circle, draw it boldly in black on a white background, and place a small dot in the centre. You can use colour if you prefer, but colour carries its own meaning, as you will have discovered if you use colour in meditation. At the moment, you want simply to respond to the circle as a shape, unhindered by other associations. Make the circle relatively large (at least 30 centimetres (1 foot) in diameter), and place it on the wall at eye-level to your seated self. Begin your meditation by focusing for a moment on your breathing, then gaze steadily at the circle. Blink when your eyes become uncomfortable, but otherwise keep blinking to a minimum.

At first, notice how your mind wants to pull away from the circle and go in search of some more 'exciting' visual stimulation. Notice it, but allow it to make no difference to your steady gazing. Notice too how all kinds of everyday associations to do with the circle will leap into your mind. Allow them to come and go, as you do with any other thoughts. Observe them but pay no particular attention to them. They are simply the attempt by your mind to make 'sense' of what you are seeing. You are not interested in this attempt, because you are focusing on the circle itself, not on ideas about circles. As your meditation deepens, profounder insights will start to emerge. Don't become excited by them. Simply observe them, as you do with more trivial thoughts. They will come back to mind again after the meditation if they are worth preserving. Don't allow yourself to feel you are meditating in order to discover some profound secret. You are meditating on the circle because it is a circle and because you are meditating, nothing more, nothing less.

After some practice in this meditation you will notice that the circle is having its own effect upon your life. It may be helping you towards an awareness of greater tranquillity in daily affairs. It may be influencing your dream life. It may be giving you insights into your self that you had not thought possible. These things are for you to discover. It is of no value for me to dictate expectations to you. These will simply get in the way of your journey.

Other geometric shapes which you can use are the cross and the triangle. Both of these also figure prominently in religious symbolism down through the centuries. The cross traditionally symbolizes the point of communication between heaven and earth; it also variously symbolizes the universal man, the tree of life, infinite expansion on all planes, male and female, the union of opposites, the descent of spirit into matter, the four rivers of paradise, the four elements united at a fifth central point.

The traditional symbolism associated with the triangle is usually concerned with the threefold nature of the universe (heaven, earth, and humankind), for example the celestial trinity which occurs in both Christianity and Hinduism, the triple jewel of Buddhism (Buddha, dharma and sangha), and the Egyptian triad of Osiris, Isis and Horus. In many spiritual and esoteric traditions, an upward-pointing triangle represents the sun and male energy, a downward pointing triangle the moon and female. Three triangles combined together form a star, the symbolism of highest attainment, the messenger of God, the presence of divinity (as in the Hebrew star of David).

These three shapes, the circle the cross and the triangle, have been combined in a number of ways by the various traditions. For example the circle enclosing the cross has often been taken to represent the union of heaven and earth, the circle at the centre of the cross solar power and majesty, and the triangle in the circle the plane of forms held within the circle of eternity. The square, which carries symbolic meaning variously as the earth, as the manifestation of God in creation, as power over all directions, as the four elements and their union, and as integrity, morality, immutability and integration, is also sometimes added to these combinations.

You can work on these shapes yourself, combining them in various different ways until you find something that seems to have direct meaning for you personally. How will you know when this meaning arises? Look for a particular sense of harmony, of balance, of an arrangement of forms which in the first instance may 'simply' carry aesthetic satisfaction. Then move forward from there.

MANDALAS AND YANTRAS

You will find examples of the arrangement of the four forms mentioned above in the patterns known respectively as 'mandalas' and 'yantras'. There is no clear distinction between these two terms. Yantras are in fact simply the form the mandala takes in Tantric practices (particular Hindu and Buddhist practices in which the emphasis is upon the transformation rather than the subjection of negative emotions). Both mandalas and yantras are usually based upon the circle (the word 'mandala' in fact means 'disc' in Sanskrit), but whereas mandalas often contain representational figures of gods, humans or animals, yantras are more usually purely geometric in design. The psychologist Carl Jung noticed how his patients, when they reached a certain stage in their psychotherapy, would often dream their own mandalas,

Figure 4   The Sricakra (Sri yantra)

and he encouraged them to paint or draw these, and then to meditate upon them for the lessons which they taught on the inner life. His own house at Bolingen in Switzerland was itself based upon the circular form, and he considered that as one advances in self-knowledge and understanding, one is moved to add to one's personal mandala until ultimately it comes to symbolize the wholeness and completeness of one's psychological and spiritual life.

One of the best-known yantras is the Sri yantra or Sricakra (wheel of Sri) shown in Figure 4. The dot at the very centre represents the origin of all things, the original point of energy. Energy makes its first movement into form by means of the female down-pointing triangle which surrounds it. From the union of energy and femininity a series of interwoven triangles emerge, four male pointing upwards, four female pointing downwards. Their interpenetration produces lesser triangles, which symbolize the subdividing of creative energy into the '10,000 things' (the specific forces which give rise to the myriad phenomena of existence). The two outer circles with their two rings of lotus petals symbolize the unfolding of these phenomena.

The Sricakra is thus a kind of symbolic 'map' (and maps are very useful on a journey) of creation. But note that each aspect of the creation which it symbolizes exists in the same space-time. Unlike more conventional Western representations, such as the time chart, it shows reality not as forming a linear progression of events, each following on after the other, but as forming part of a simultaneous reality, as forming part of the 'All time is forever present' world offered us by the poet T. S. Eliot.

If you use a mandala or a yantra such as the Sricakra, remember however that you mustn't *impose* this interpretation upon its symbolism. If you do, then you are simply thinking *about* the symbolism rather than experiencing what it represents. Instead, allow your mind to go into the yantra, first by flowing with the movement from the centre outwards, and then by flowing from the outside back into the centre. Travel slowly. Try not to move the eyes, but to take in the whole pattern from the one point of vision. Don't think of words even like 'triangle' or 'circle' to describe this journey. Simply follow the shapes.

And as I said when discussing the circle, don't in any case be bounded by the interpretations I've just given. The yantra will reveal meaning to you in other ways. Allow this meaning to arise in its own time and in its own manner. And allow the direct experience of the yantra, with its intermingling of symbolic shapes, to work its own 'magic' in introducing a harmony and a balance into your life which you may become increasingly aware of as time goes by, yet without quite knowing how it has been achieved.

USING INNER VISION

I indicated earlier that you can travel with pictures not only by observing them directly but by holding them in the mind as visualizations. Visualization is in fact a very powerful psychological tool in its own right. In both the spiritual and the magical traditions, it has indeed been frequently regarded as one of the practices essential to progress. Both the Tibetan monk and the Western sorcerer's apprentice had to undergo a lengthy training in the art of visualization. Certain modern psychotherapeutic systems, such as psychosynthesis, also make extensive use of it. Even modern medicine, as in the work for example of the Simontons, is now coming to realize the extent to which appropriate visualizations can help the body to heal itself (a point to which I return later in this chapter).

If you are one of those people who claim to have little visual imagination (since this is what visualization involves), be reassured. Everyone can visualize, and visualize so realistically that they mistake their own creations for reality. We each of us do it every night in dreams. And if you're someone who claims never to dream, be re assured again. We each of us dream every night, and although some of us never remember our dreams the following morning, with training we can quite readily come to do so.

The reason some of us find it hard to visualize while we are awake is twofold. Firstly we run up against the old problem of our inability to stay concentrated for any length of time on any one thing. And secondly we run up against the problem of insufficient practice. Unlike previous generations, we have virtually no need to visualize in normal life. Everything is done for us. We are surrounded by images in books, on posters, on films, on the television. Whenever we go sightseeing we carry our cameras around as if attached to us by umbilical cords. We never have to remember how things look, we simply take photographs of them. And when we aren't taking photographs we're busy buying picture postcards or glossy souvenir books. Before the advent of the camera, people either remembered what they saw, or else they took their sketchbooks or their watercolours with them and created their own pictures (in itself a potent method for fixing scenes in the memory and thus training our visualization powers).

The result of our lack of visualization practice is that although we're quite good at remembering words (though not as good as the monks and storytellers of old, who would learn thousands upon thousands of words of scriptures and narratives and repeat them word perfect), we're lost when it comes to remembering visual images. And visual images, as I said when discussing symbols a short while ago, often provide us with much more powerful keys to our inner psychological landscape than does spoken language.

If you are working with a mandala or a yantra, try after a time to commit it to visual memory so completely that you see it in your mind's eye as clearly as if it hangs on the wall in front of you. In this way the image becomes internalized, as if the boundaries between you and it have disappeared, and it gains in potency accordingly.

Develop your powers of visualization by gazing first at a simple shape, such as the circle or the square or the cross. Gaze at it steadily, without making any attempt to commit it to memory. Then suddenly snap the eyes shut, and hold the image behind your closed eyelids, almost as if you have taken a photograph of it. Don't worry if the colours change from the real image 'out there'. The shape is what matters. Hold it in your mind for as long as you can, but without making too fierce an effort. If it drifts away to one side or the other, bring it gently back into the centre. When the image fades, open your eyes and gaze steadily at it once more, then when you feel ready close them and repeat the exercise.

Before very long, you will find that you are able to visualize the shape at will as soon as you close your eyes, even without first gazing at it. Then practise with another shape, and then another. Once you can visualize several shapes easily, play about with them in your mind's eye, combining them and separating them as you please. If by now you can also visualize colours readily, give the shapes colours, and then change the colours. Work towards the point at which the visualization becomes effortless, and stays at the centre of your visual imagination without wandering off or growing less symmetrical or less distinct. Then and only then, go back to your mandala or your yantra, and start to work with that in the same way.

TRAVELLING WITH PUZZLES

The human mind is naturally curious; so there is something about a puzzle that sets most of us thinking. We're intrigued to know the answer, and often we worry away at it until we find what that answer is. A puzzle therefore is often a good way of getting us to concentrate, to focus our minds, to start a process not unlike that of meditation.

The difference between this process and meditation is, however, that when solving a puzzle we follow our thoughts instead of just observing them. We pick up one train of thinking after another. We use our rational, logical minds. We assume there must be a solution, and by sifting the evidence, by fitting together the various pieces of information contained in the puzzle, and by calling on our existing knowledge, we hope to be able to arrive at it.

But what happens if our rational, logical minds don't get us anywhere? What happens if the pieces of information contained in the puzzle not only fail to fit together but actively contradict each other? What happens if there is nothing in our store of knowledge that allows us to see why this is and what we should be doing about it? What then?

Maybe we give up. Maybe we decide the puzzle is a waste of time, and that the answer, if answer there be, must forever remain a mystery to us. Or maybe we keep at it. Maybe the puzzle so intrigues us that it begins to take a hold on our mind. Maybe we find ourselves constantly returning to it, becoming obsessed, even haunted by it. Maybe we go on and on, trying solution after solution after solution, and finding that each one, no matter how much it excites us at the time, fails to fit. Finally, in exasperation, in desperation, in near total despair, we. . . what? What happens then?

In the Rinzai school of Zen Buddhism, such puzzles are known as 'koans'. The Zen teacher gives the pupil a koan, selected especially for him or her. The pupil goes away, and begins searching for the solution. After a time (hours, days, weeks) a solution comes, and the pupil hurries to tell the teacher. The teacher listens to the solution, gives a shake of the head, and sends the pupil away to work harder. The pupil is told to meditate on the koan, to focus on it in much the same way that one focuses on the breath or on a mandala, to repeat the koan over and over again like a mantra, but with the difference that now one is responding not only to the sound but to the puzzle contained in the sound.

One is told to work on this puzzle with total, single-minded determination, sometimes actively seeking, sometimes simply holding the koan in the mind and waiting to see what comes. But don't, says the contemporary Zen teacher Master Sheng-Yen, 'try to reason out an answer. You'll never get it that way. You must work on it as if chewing on nails. You must use it to form in your mind a hot ball of doubt that will drive you to find the answer'. And when the answer comes, the pupil may express it in words, or in gestures, or even in silence. Only the teacher is able to recognize whether the answer is acceptable or not, since such answers are not 'standard' in the way that answers on an examination paper may be standard, and pupils may not always give this answer in what outwardly appears to be the same way.

Sometimes these answers can in fact seem so strange that the dialogue between the teacher and the pupil may appear to be what Sheng-Yen calls 'a dialogue between insane, or at least eccentric people'. Because, and this is where words are not necessarily that much help, the answer (perhaps we should say the *resolution*) of the koan comes at the point where the mind is driven beyond its rational, 'normal' way of conceptualizing and labelling and categorizing the world. The point at which the mind is driven in fact to experience things directly, without the obscurity which the intellect, for all its undoubted value, can place like a veil between us and what actually is.

It is said that through the resolution of koans, Zen can thus take us in a single leap into insight, instead of leaving us first to work through the stages of concentration and tranquillity. It is thus a shortcut on our journey, though there are very few who are able to take it.

There is a sense in which the haikus I mentioned earlier (Chapter 4) can give us an inkling of what the resolution of a koan is actually 'like', because haikus carry a direct pointing at reality. In their few short syllables they provide for us a sudden insight into the heart of an experience, rather than leaving us wrapped up in mere appearances. Zen art, where the painter captures the essence of something in a few deft strokes (the 'catness' of a cat, the 'treeness' of a tree, the 'rockness' of a rock) gives us a further hint.

One of the best-known koans, and one which has a particular appeal to the Western mind, is the one I mentioned in Chapter 4, 'What is the sound of one hand clapping?' What indeed? What can be the sound of one hand, if by definition clapping is caused by two hands? Could the answer be silence? Hardly, since the koan indicates that 'clapping' is taking place. Well then, can the hand be clapping against itself? If so, could that really be called clapping? And so one goes on. Until one realizes that perhaps this isn't the way one should be travelling at all. In which case, is there another direction? If so, where is it? Or is the whole idea of 'direction' wrong as well? And is another contemporary Zen teacher, Master Seung Sahn, right to keep emphasizing the old Zen saying that always we must keep a 'don't know' mind?

Many of the best-known koans confuse us even further in that they are given to us with both the question and a resolution, as for example in the koan 'Mu'. In this koan we are told that when asked by a monk if a dog has buddha-nature (i.e. the potential for enlightenment) the Zen Master Joshu answered 'Mu', which literally means 'not' or 'none'. Another example is the answer 'Three bundles of flax', which the Master Tozan gave to the monk who asked him 'Who is the Buddha?'. Another is Ummon's answer, 'As high as Mount Sumeru' when asked 'When no thought is stirring in the mind, is there error there?'

Presented with one of these koans, the pupil is now expected by the teacher to struggle with the *resolutions* rather than with the original questions. What do these resolutions mean? Can one make any kind of sense out of them, and how do they fit the question? If 'Mu' simply means 'not' or 'none', why should this be a koan? Surely Joshu's answer is a straightforward negative. Yet if it is, what does 'not' or 'none' really represent? Or what did Joshu intend it to represent? In some of the most extensive collections of koans such as the *Mumonkan* or the *Hekiganroku* (poetically translated respectively as *The Gateless Gate* and the *Blue Cliff Record*) the student is not only given the question and the resolution, but also an introduction to them both *and* commentaries upon them appended by other Zen masters over the centuries (and sometimes, if you please, commentaries upon the commentaries!). Intended to be helpful, these introductions and commentaries often produce at first sight only added confusion.

I'll give one of the shortest and least obviously bizarre examples from the *Blue Cliff Record*.

Introduction
When the action of the mind is stopped and swept away the iron tree will bloom. Can you demonstrate it? Even a crafty fellow will come a cropper here. Even if he excels in every way, he will have his nostrils pierced. Where are the complications? See the following.

Main Subject
Riku Taifu, while talking with Nansen, said 'Jo Hosshi said "Heaven and earth and I are all of the same substance". Isn't that absolutely fantastic?' Nansen pointed to a flower in the garden, called Taifu to him and said 'People of these days see this flower as though they were in dream'.

Commentary
Hearing, seeing and touching are not one and one. Mountains and rivers should not be viewed in the mirror. The frosty sky, the setting moon – at midnight; With whom will the serene waters of the lake reflect the shadows in the cold?

The Introduction sounds rather like the clue in a crossword puzzle. The Main Subject sounds like a simple statement that people don't really see things properly. And the Commentary sounds like an attempt in poetry at contradicting Jo Hosshi's statement contained in the Main Subject. But as the Zen master would say if you offered these solutions to him or her, 'If you think that, you are wrong. And if you don't think that, you are wrong. Now *answer*!' And if he or she was so minded, we'd probably be given a ritual slap across the shoulders just for emphasis.

As D. T. Suzuki puts it, the koan is designed 'to exclude the intellect, and to lead our empirical consciousness to its deeper sources', whether we label these sources 'the Unknown, the Beyond, the Unconscious' or whatever. The Zen master 'has no deliberate scheme. . . to make his statements. . . uncouth or logically unpalatable; the statements come forth from his inner being, as flowers burst out in Springtime or as the sun sheds its rays'.

Something of this 'bursting forth' is expressed by Tozan (again in *The Blue Cliff Record*), whose enlightenment came to him, after long study, on seeing his shadow cast on the water while wading across a stream.

> Long seeking it through others,
> I was far from reaching it,
> Now I go by myself;
> I meet it everywhere.
> It is just I by myself,
> And I am not itself.
> Understanding this way,
> I can be as I am.

OPEN-EYE MEDITATION

Working with one's koan is a form of open-eye meditation. One works with it while going about one's ordinary life, while eating, while working, while preparing for sleep. And of course one also works with it in meditation, which in the Zen tradition is usually done with the eyes open or slightly open, facing the wall in the Soto Zen tradition and facing out into the room in the Rinzai.

In Zen, the meditation practice is termed 'zazen', and in the course of it one first achieves *joriki* ('mental strength' arising from one-pointedness of mind) followed by *shi* ('stopping' – a calm state in which the wavering mind becomes steady and clear), and then consequent upon *shi* one attains *kan* ('view' – an objective awareness in which things are seen just as they are). The parallels between *joriki*, *shi* and *kan* on the one hand, and concentration, tranquillity and insight on the other, need no emphasis.

93

As in vipassana, the initial practice in zazen is to work with the breathing, but eventually one graduates to the koan or to *shikan-taza*, in the latter of which there is no specific point of focus but in which the meditator is keenly aware of whatever goes on around him or her, and also of what goes on within the mind. *Shikan-taza* is thus a state of total watchful awareness, an awareness in which, as the Buddhist sutra puts it:

> In what is seen there must be just the seen;
> In what is sensed there must be just the sensed;
> In what is thought there must be just the thought.

Zen also teaches 'kinhin', walking meditation. In kinhin, the meditator walks deliberately and mindfully and with eyes open but lowered, placing each foot a measured distance in front of the other, and fully conscious of each action of the body and of each sensation associated with it. In many ways the effect of this is similar to the practice of allowing the awareness to 'sweep' the body as mentioned on page 63. In addition, intense concentration on the movement of the body and the stillness of the mind – and on the similarities and differences between the two – helps the meditator gain further insight into his or her own being in all its aspects.

Another example of open-eyed meditation is the Tibetan Buddhist practice of 'shi-ne'. Like all the other techniques mentioned so far, shi-ne is concerned with stilling the mind, and thus allowing it to gain insight. The eyes are open, but focused on empty space about a metre (a few feet) in front of the face rather than upon a mandala or upon a blank wall. Initially, as in vipassana, the focus of attention is upon the breath, but rather than focusing upon the nostrils or the abdomen the meditator is told to 'find the presence of awareness' in his or her breathing, a rather more subtle teaching. Without a specific physical location upon which to focus, the meditator becomes aware just of 'breathing', of the essence if you like of breathing, rather than of the physical sensations associated with it.

Through shi-ne, the meditator gains insight into *emptiness*, an important concept in all forms of Buddhist meditation. Emptiness, if it can be explained at all in words, is the 'no-*thing*-ness' from which *things* emerge, the unconditioned energy from which the world of forms arises. This is an important realization, and one which has interesting parallels with the view of the modern atomic physicist that all matter is fundamentally not 'stuff' at all but is composed of energy, an energy without definition in and of itself. Rather than simply enjoying an intellectual understanding of the complicated concept of emptiness, shi-ne allows the meditator to gain some sense of directly experiencing it.

Having gained insight into emptiness through shi-ne, the meditator is then aware of thoughts, sensations, ideas, arising out of this emptiness and taking form within the mind. Known as lha-tong, this realization allows us to see how form is constantly being created from emptiness, only to disappear back into emptiness again. A constant stream of energy flowing from emptiness and coalescing into form, only to stream back once more into emptiness. Finally, in what is called nyi-med, the meditator becomes aware of both emptiness and form at the same time, and of their non-dual nature. That is, the meditator experiences the fact that as form comes exclusively from emptiness and emptiness comes exclusively from form, there can in essence be no distinction between the two. Emptiness is form, and form is emptiness. Neither is 'superior' or 'inferior' to the other. They are one and the same thing, and it is only our unenlightened way of 'seeing' that leads us to believe in a distinction between the two.

Zen Buddhism expresses this realization tellingly in the beautiful saying that:

> Before studying Zen I saw mountains as mountains and rivers as rivers. Then I began to study Zen and I saw that mountains are not mountains and rivers are not rivers. But after realizing Zen I saw once more that mountains are mountains and rivers are rivers.

You come full circle, and appear to be back at the starting point. But there is a big difference. You are in the same place yet not in the same place, because now you have the experience of seeing into the true nature of mountains and rivers. You have travelled round the circle. You have realized 'why' mountains are mountains and rivers are rivers. It is, to go

BOX 7
EMPTINESS AND ENLIGHTENMENT

In any discussion of meditation, and particularly when concepts like 'emptiness' are mentioned, people are apt to ask about enlightenment. Does meditation lead to enlightenment? And if so, how does one recognize this enlightenment when it comes?

I've emphasized several times that one doesn't have a 'goal' in meditation, because the existence of such a goal is to prejudge the issue. It assumes we already 'know' this goal, or at least know what it looks like. But those who meditate for spiritual reasons quite reasonably feel that enlightenment is bound up in some way with meditation, and that the concept is at least in the back of their minds if nowhere else.

So what is enlightenment? Edwin Arnold in *The Light of Asia* tells us that:

> The nature of the mind when understood
> No human words can compass or disclose,
> Enlightenment is nought to be obtained
> And he that finds it does not say he knows.

A timely warning. But there is no warning against looking for a clue. And that clue is given to us in the third stage of the meditation practice, *insight*. Enlightenment is insight into reality, the direct experience of things as they are. What else could it be?

This means that instead of thinking of enlightenment as a single blinding flash of revelation (though of course it could be that), it may be more helpful to think of it as a step-by-step process, a number of *enlightenment experiences*. As we gain insight into the physical body, into the emotions, into the mind, and into the emptiness from which form emerges and into which form returns, we are progressively going deeper and deeper into a direct experience of reality, an experience which may bring us in time to a profound spiritual realization of the nature of our own existence and of the existence of all other created things.

But if we set out deliberately to achieve this realization, then our very *deliberateness*, with all the mental concepts that it contains, and our very preoccupation with *achievement*, may serve as the barriers which come between it and us.

back to the words of T. S. Eliot, to be in the same place, 'and to know it for the first time'.

Lha-tong and nyi-med are therefore components of the insight stage of meditation, an insight which embraces both the world 'out there' and the world 'in here'. In realizing them, one comes closer to realizing the nature not only of the world but of one's own being.

OPEN-EYE VERSUS CLOSED-EYE MEDITATION

Meditating with open eyes helps to keep you in touch with this world instead of withdrawing too far into yourself, but closing the eyes has the advantage of developing more rapidly your insight into your own nature. However, whether the path is inner or outer, it leads in the same direction, so neither method is 'better' than the other. Decide on the method that seems right for you, and keep that at the centre of your practice. But use the other method too from time to time. Your meditation should enable you to explore both inner and outer space.

CONTEMPLATION

This section would not be complete without some reference to contemplation, a practice which, among Western Christians in particular, is often confused with meditation. Contemplation carries different meanings for different people but essentially it involves an inner thought process centred around some important concept or article of faith or moral precept. For example, one could contemplate such statements as 'God is love', or one of the ten commandments or Buddhist precepts. The mind examines the statement from every point of view, endeavouring to obtain insight into its true meaning. Each time the mind wonders too far, it is brought gently back to the statement itself.

Such a practice differs importantly from meditation in that it can be characterized by identification with one's thought processes or with one's emotional responses, rather than by observation of them. However, contemplation is a very valuable practice in and of itself, and can lead not only to a fuller understanding of the statement contemplated but also to sudden flashes of profound insight. As I said earlier, we must never devalue thought itself simply because in meditation we are freeing ourselves from over-control by thought and experiencing the underlying reality from which thought arises. Thought is a powerful and vital tool of the mind, and only causes us problems when we assume that it *is* the mind.

You may wonder nevertheless how contemplation differs from koan meditation, which also takes its starting point from a statement. The difference is that in koan meditation we are working with a statement that is ultimately paradoxical, and which we are trying in some sense to 'resolve'. And to do so, moreover, without the use of thought or emotion. We may certainly begin with thought and/or with emotion, but there comes a point where these drop away, and the answer comes as a moment of pure experience, which we express spontaneously and directly. Each time the koan is put to us, this moment of experience arises as if it has never left us (as indeed it has not). In contemplation on the other hand, the aim is usually to work *by means of* thought and emotion. Sometimes these may in fact drop away, leaving us in a state of intuitive 'knowing' much as in meditation, but this is not necessarily our intention.

It's also true that whereas meditation involves a relatively specific set of practices, contemplation is a state into which we enter whenever we ponder the meaning of a statement by an advanced teacher, or the line of a poem, or the atmosphere captured by a painting or by a piece of music. It does not usually involve either the 'discipline' inseparable from meditation, or the consistent use of the same point of focus.

DISTRACTIONS IN MEDITATION

From the start of your meditation, you will experience distractions. Few meditators ever become completely free from them. And the fact that we seem to be able to ignore them in one meditation is no guarantee we'll be able to ignore them next time around. In fact this up and down nature of meditation can be a major distraction in itself. We seem to be making good progress for a session or two, and feel that we have at last learnt how to keep our mind still and calm, and the next day (often for no apparent reason) we find we can hardly concentrate for two minutes together. We become frustrated with ourselves, and disenchanted with meditation, and these angry feelings are a further barrier between us and what we are trying to do.

The golden rule is always just to sit through whatever comes up. Without realizing it, we often make more progress during those meditations where we have to work hard to stay concentrated than in those where concentration comes easily. And if frustration at what you see as your own incompetence arises, simply observe it as you observe everything else in meditation.

'Simply observe it' is in fact the way to deal with all distractions. People naturally ask what should they do when the noise of traffic in the streets, or of the television next door, or of children playing in the garden intrude into their tranquillity. Equally they ask what should they do when legs start to ache, when noses start to itch, when a foot goes to sleep, when the tune of a popular song maddeningly starts playing over and over again in the brain. The answer each time can only be 'simply observe it'.

This is more easily said than done of course. But you can see the truth of it when you remind yourself that meditation is not an 'escape' from reality. It is a looking at, an enquiry into, reality. And the distractions both outside and inside the mind are part of that reality. They are not 'separate' from you. They are part of your life-experience in the moment in which they register upon your senses. Sense-experience is an integral part of being alive, not some additional extra like a blanket thrown over bare shoulders.

So don't try and ignore distractions, don't try and push them away. But equally, don't react to them. Accept them as part of the flow of experience that has its being in and through us. When meditating with a teacher in certain forms of the shi-ne practice mentioned earlier, he or she lets out a fierce and penetrating yell, or smacks two pieces of wood together like a pistol shot at certain unpredictable points. These intrusions into one's meditation come violently, almost brutally. When

I first experienced them, my whole body seemed to vibrate inwardly for moments afterwards. The sound tears into the meditator, deliberately shattering his or her tranquillity into a thousand pieces.

Or does it? Is tranquillity really shattered? If it is, then it isn't true tranquillity. The abrupt explosion of sound from the teacher is actually an act of great kindness on his or her part. What is being tested is the level of the meditator's tranquillity. If the meditator has been shut off into a cosy inner world, imagining it to be tranquillity, the impact of the sound quickly brings disillusion. If one jumps out of one's skin, one certainly wasn't in a state of tranquillity. But if one was, then the sound is accepted by the mind simply as a sound, a sound which helps the meditator to see more deeply into the true nature of experience.

So although in the early days of your meditation practice you may find it necessary to have silence around you, as you progress you will become more and more able to sit with extraneous noises, recognizing them as part of your mind (or, if you prefer, as part of what is happening in your mind). But this still leaves the problem of the pain in the leg or the itch on the nose or the pins and needles in the foot. What do you do? Shift into a more comfortable position? Scratch the nose? Rub the foot back into life?

It isn't a crime to do any of these things. You should never turn your meditation into a trial, which has to be endured with grim determination come what may. But the stillness of the body *is* important, since it helps to still the mind. Also important is the realization that if you are uncomfortable now and shift to ease your discomfort, you will feel just as uncomfortable again in a few minutes. Further, by attempting to 'escape' from your discomfort, you are missing the opportunity to learn from it. We spend a great deal of our lives trying to make things 'comfortable' for ourselves, and then becoming frustrated or frightened or angry when they refuse to fit in with our plans. In meditation you have the opportunity to learn how to adapt to discomfort, to see that it is perfectly possible to remain in equanimity even when things are not just as you would have them be.

So sit through your discomfort if you can. Don't try and push it away. Don't try and ignore it. But on the other hand, don't concentrate on it either. Concentrating on it only gives it added importance (concentrating on an itch on the nose for example can quickly seem to drive you to distraction). Note it, observe it, see what the physical sensation actually *is* (as opposed to giving it a label or judging it in some way), and continue with your practice.

Eventually, your meditation will embrace all these distractions, seeing them, like extraneous noises, as part of the moment by moment flow of experience. At that point they will cease to be distractions, and become part of a pattern, a pattern that is made up of many shapes and many colours but is ultimately a unity embracing both inner and outer worlds, complete in and of itself.

MEDITATION IN DAILY LIFE

I have stressed many times that meditation isn't an escape from reality, but a way of dealing with it, of gaining insight into it. This being the case, meditation shouldn't be confined just to those times when you can sit and practice. Meditation should be something that can be carried through into daily life, even reaching the point where life itself becomes a meditation. If this sounds impossibly over-idealistic, or as if you are expected to go through life like a monk or nun, rest assured. It's nothing of the kind. It means only that you will be able to bring something of the concentration, the relaxed focused attention that characterizes your sitting practice, into the wider business of living.

As I've said earlier, much of the time we go through our lives in a kind of dream, our minds always on something other than what we are actually doing. This leads variously to reduced efficiency, to unnecessary levels of stress, to torpor, and to forgetfulness (for example the annoying 'I had it in my hands a moment ago, now *where* did I put it?' syndrome). The lessons learnt in meditation help us to counteract this. They help us to put our minds in the moment, to be in the here and now, to experience life directly instead of being lost in the distractions of thoughts, memories, expectations, intentions, that come like a fuzzy screen between us and living.

Much of this increased concentration comes naturally once we take up the practice of meditation, especially if we use exercises like Exercise 5 in the last chapter. But it can be encouraged by reminding ourselves as often as possible during our waking hours to observe what is happening to us and around us in much the way that we observe phenomena in meditation. This practice, known as 'mindfulness', is the exact opposite of absent-mindedness. It doesn't mean that we should never settle into internal reveries. It means that we should always know what it is we are doing. If we want, as a conscious decision, to go into reverie that is fine. Reverie can be very helpful. But we don't sink into it inadvertently, habitually, as is so often the case.

A simple technique for helping you with the practice of mindfulness is to keep up an internal running commentary on what it is you are doing. This makes you concentrate, makes you put your mind in your actions, makes you notice things around you, makes you properly aware and attentive. If you're forced to break off one action halfway through in order to start on something else, it records the fact for you, and helps you remember where you were in the first action. The result is that you can return to this action as soon as possible and pick it up again at the point at which you left it. The internal commentary keys you into life, instead of leaving you to go through it with your consciousness on automatic pilot.

Try this running commentary for a few minutes at a time, several times a day. Allow it to include awareness of your own thoughts and feelings as you react to what is going on around you. Try it when you are harassed and attempting to do 101 things at once. Try it when you are out walking or driving, so that it makes you use your eyes and take in the things around you. Try it when you're engaged on a particularly boring task like washing dishes, and when the mind is prone to go wandering off on its own. It will help train your mind, so that after a time you will find yourself paying more attention to life even when the commentary isn't going on inside your head.

The development of mindfulness helps you be more

effective and better organized. But it does more than that. It continues the process of insight that you are developing in your sitting meditation. It helps you become more aware of what it is to be alive, of the nature of reality, of the moment by moment ebb and flow of events in the outside world and of the moment by moment ebb and flow of your reactions to them. It is no accident that so many of the great spiritual traditions place emphasis upon mindfulness, from the frequent admonitions in the gospels to 'watch' to the clarion call of 'awake' that runs through much Islamic literature.

The Buddhist *Dhammapada* has an especially telling way of putting it:

> Watchfulness is the path of immortality: unwatchfulness is the path of death. Those who are watchful never die: those who do not watch are already as dead.

Food for thought there all right.

ACHIEVING SPECIFIC GOALS

I discussed earlier in this chapter the way in which you can use simple visualization as a point of focus in meditation. Once you have developed your ability both to concentrate and to visualize clearly, you can use visualization in other ways too. When doing so you depart from your usual meditation practice in that you are now setting out to achieve specific, clearly defined and predetermined goals. Use the exercises as an adjunct to your usual meditation practice, not in place of it.

The psychological principle behind these exercises is relatively easy to understand, and confirms that their regular use can be very effective indeed. Let's explain this principle by taking the example of someone suffering from a bad back. The nagging pain and the restriction of movement caused by the problem quickly lead the sufferer to think of him or herself as a person moving slowly and stiffly through life, constantly on the defence against anything that could make matters worse. Their self-image in consequence becomes that of a person with a bad back. At both conscious and unconscious levels, they no longer think of themselves as someone who can move freely and confidently.

The result of this negative self-image is that the individual sees him or herself in terms of disability rather than ability. Not only does this have a depressing psychological effect (in itself an obstacle to recovery), it results in the body becoming full of tension, the opposite of what is required if healing is to take place. A simple visualization exercise, carried out for a few minutes once or twice a day, as an adjunct to appropriate medical treatment, helps combat this self-defeating state of affairs. In the exercise, the individual pictures him or herself free from pain once more, and, with full mobility restored to the back, moving with the relaxed freedom of old.

With the help of this visualization, both the conscious and the unconscious mind develop a self-image of health rather than of ill-health. The body is helped to let go of tensions, the mind to become more optimistic, and the processes of healing are given an important boost. Even modern medicine, which has long held out against a full recognition of the role played by the mind in physical health, is now coming to accept that the way we think affects the way we are.

Visualizations can help psychologically and spiritually as well as physically. Just as a negative physical self-image interferes with physical well-being, so a negative psychological self-image interferes with psychological well-being. If we constantly think of ourselves as shy for example, or as depressed or over-anxious, then we are conditioning ourselves to be shy or depressed or over-anxious. We need to replace unsatisfactory self-images of this kind with positive ones which actually contain the person we want to be.

Spiritually, we can also help by visualizing ourselves as possessing those qualities we need for our further development. Buddhism teaches practices in which the meditator visualizes in minute detail every aspect of an image of the Buddha (or of some other spiritual teacher), building up the image from the lotus throne upon which the Buddha sits to the position of the arms and hands, to the garments, and to the expression of compassion and serenity on the face. The image symbolizes for the meditator the psychological and spiritual qualities he or she wishes to develop, and when the visualization is so stabilized that it stands out as clearly in the mind as if it were objectively present, the meditator visualizes these desirable qualities as streaming in rays of white light into his or her own being. Finally, the image itself is dissolved into this white light, which is visualized (and felt) as entering the meditator's head and flowing down through the body until it comes to rest in the tranquillity of the heart.

Frequent use of this meditation has a positive and profound effect upon the spiritual development of the meditator. If you want a psychological explanation, this is because the image of the Buddha becomes one's self-image. One comes to see oneself as possessing the qualities which the Buddha represents, and these qualities (latent in us all) are then encouraged at both conscious and unconscious levels to develop more fully. However, you may wish for a spiritual explanation over and above this, namely that through visualizations of this kind we not only work more effectively on ourselves but also receive the intangible gift of grace which lies at the heart of the spiritual vision.

VISUALIZATION TECHNIQUES

There are many different ways in which you can use visualizations for physical, psychological or spiritual purposes, and many books available which explain them to you. But the principle behind them all is relatively simple. Use your visual imagination to create a picture of what it is you want to become. The clearer and more convincing the picture, and the more closely you identify with it, the more likely are you to achieve the desired results.

In the case of physical problems, the aim therefore is to visualize yourself as free of these problems, or to visualize yourself as fighting and defeating them. If you have a skin condition, the visualization will involve visualizing your skin clear and smooth again. If you have breathing problems, the visualization will be of yourself breathing freely and easily. If you have an internal problem, the visualization will be of your immune system (which you can symbolize in any way that appeals to you – white light, an army of white soldiers, a healing river) fighting and destroying it. The visualization can be of two main kinds:

- an outer visualization, such as yourself running joyfully and pain free along a beach or through a wood or wherever you choose
- an inner visualization, such as your white blood corpuscles defeating an infection, or torn muscles or ligaments healing.

In addition you can 'feel' yourself moving freely or in whatever state it is you want to achieve. Identify fully with the feeling. Imagine yourself becoming one with the 'objective' visualization of yourself running along the beach, and sensing the joy of movement as if it is actually happening to you, here and now, in this moment. Exercise 7 gives a brief example, using a bad back as the point of focus.

EXERCISE 7

This exercise can be carried out lying down (though you can sit in your meditation position if you prefer). Keep the mind alert, just as usual.

Allow the body to relax. Let your awareness sweep the body, as in meditation, letting go of any tensions which you may find. Now create an image of a peaceful scene, say a sandy beach. Keep the visualization simple. Concentrate upon the long sweep of sand, upon the sea breaking in gentle waves upon the shore, on the blue sunlit sky. Now visualize birds soaring and swooping above you. Be conscious of the freedom of their movement, of their grace and relaxed beauty.

Now visualize a human figure, yourself, in light clothing or naked, running and dancing with the same freedom and grace along the shoreline. See your feet throwing up a spray of water that sparkles in the sun. Notice how pain free and unrestricted you are, how your body can leap and twist and turn as it pleases.

Now put your consciousness inside that body, so that you feel this freedom from inside. Feel the sun on your body, the sand and the water beneath your feet, the warm air as you run through it, the ease with which your back allows you to do as you please, to bend and stretch, to relax into the joy of movement.

Allow this to continue for as long as you wish.

When you are ready, withdraw from the visualization, so that you are lying once more in your room but still feeling the freedom and sheer exhilaration of movement in your body. Then dissolve the visualization of the scene in front of you, allowing the running figure and the sea and the sky and the beach to be absorbed into you rather than vanish. Tell yourself that you will be able to return to the scene whenever you want.

Don't be tempted to leap up now as if you back has received instant healing. Behave sensibly, but keep the feeling of relaxation in the muscles and nerves of the back, and the realization that healing is taking place. Nature knows her own business best. Once we give her the chance, she will do the healing for us.

Adapt the principles of this exercise for any other physical or psychological problem with which you happen to be working. But never use them as a substitute for seeking properly qualified medical advice. They are additional to such advice, not an alternative to it.

The procedure outlined in Exercise 7 is similar when used for psychological problems. For example, use an outer 'objective' visualization to see yourself coping confidently with a situation that has previously proved difficult for you. Visualize the situation in as much detail as you can. Visualize the other people who may be there, and 'hear' what they are likely to say. Now imagine yourself identifying with and moving inside the visualization of your confident self, so that you and it become one, and you feel the relaxed energy with which this self is dealing with the problem. Alternatively if you're depressed, visualize yourself in good spirits (talking to friends, taking a favourite walk), and then merge with this high-spirited self or allow it to merge with you.

If you are using visualization as a spiritual practice allow it to take the form of the Buddhist meditation I've already described, visualizing Christ or any other religious or exemplary figure in place of the Buddha if you prefer. Be careful not to hurry the visualization. Build it up slowly, and according to the same set pattern each time. The more care and attention you pay to this, the more you impress upon your conscious and unconscious mind that everything connected with the practice is important and must be taken deeply to heart.

As with all work of this kind, never be impatient. We're so conditioned to expect quick results (a magic pill that will put everything to rights) that we anticipate experiencing the desired effects after only a few minutes of visualization. You will need to work for twenty minutes a day for some time (weeks, perhaps months) before the benefits will begin to show. Even then, success isn't guaranteed. Or it may come in an unexpected form. For example, you may find you begin to understand your physical disability or your psychological problem better, to understand why it is there and what it is perhaps trying to teach you. Or you may find yourself more tolerant of it, gentler and less impatient with it, better able to cope.

Don't be discouraged if your progress seems slow. When you come to hills, progress is bound to be a little slower.

7 · GUIDES AND COMPANIONS

You will sometimes hear it said that you cannot make progress in meditation without a teacher. This is true. But perhaps not in the sense in which you at first imagine. For you are your own best teacher. Other people can help, particularly if they have trodden the path you are now treading, and know some of the snares and pitfalls. They can encourage you, listen to your accounts of progress and setbacks, advise you when to move from one practise to another, give you koans and other travellers' aids. But they cannot take your journey for you. In the end, you are the one who travels, and you are the one who must find the path.

Books can also be a help. Some meditation teachers will tell you that you can't learn from books, but these are usually teachers over-influenced by Eastern traditions, where books and their power are not always as well known and appreciated as in the West. It is true that you can't learn *just* by reading books. You must put into practice what they teach. But books are not the dry, detached, cerebral things that some critics of book learning would have us believe. Books are a dynamic communication of ideas. More, they are a dynamic communication of emotions and feelings. They can speak directly to us, sparking off latent potential in ourselves just as can any other deeply lived experience. To pretend otherwise is to dismiss the impact not just of books on meditation but also of the great books of world literature. It is to dismiss poetry, stories, and the enduring myths and legends of humankind which help us to know and explain ourselves to ourselves. It is also to dismiss the value of spiritual writings such as the Bible, the Vedas, the Upanishads, the Gita, the Sutras, and the outpourings of the Christian mystics such as Meister Eckhardt, St John of the Cross, St Teresa of Avila, Mother Julian of Norwich, and many more besides.

Books are not a substitute for practice, but then they are not meant to be. They are guides to set you on your way, travelling companions to help you recognize your path when you find it. They can motivate, arouse interest, even inspire. And by placing the onus upon yourself rather than upon a teacher physically present, they can help you to be more self-reliant, readier to explore, more aware of the personal nature of what it is you are trying to do.

So never be deterred from meditation by people who say you can't learn the practice from books. On the other hand, if you find a good teacher, he or she can answer individual queries, listen to your grumbles, help your through periods when you may not feel you are making progress, and above all enthuse you with personal example. You look at your teacher and admire his or her open, optimistic, serene approach to life, and you think that if that is what meditation can do for them, then certainly it is something worth having.

But how do you find a good teacher? Since of all the great religions Buddhism places most emphasis upon meditation, you may find one by identifying a Buddhist group near you and contacting them; the public library usually has details, or you can get the addresses of all the larger Buddhist centres from the Buddhist Society at 58 Eccleston Square, London SW1V 1PH. Or you may find a yoga teacher who takes meditation classes. Or you may wish to work through a Transcendental Meditation (TM) group, where the emphasis is upon a simple mantra meditation. But if you find the philosophy surrounding any of these groups unacceptable to you, there is no reason at all why you shouldn't continue to work on your own. An increased sympathy towards the philosophical teachings that accompany many meditational practices may develop of itself as you progress along the path, but that is for you to discover.

In my own experience of a wide range of meditation teachers over the years I have invariably found that those who helped me most were those who were open to experience rather than firmly located in one dogma or another. Perhaps this says something about meditation teachers, perhaps it says something about me. But remember, in meditation as in all of life, no one has a monopoly of the truth. And if they try to tell you they have, then avoid them and their teachings.

THE MEDITATION RETREAT

At some point, you may feel you want a more intensive experience of meditation, spread over a few days or even weeks. This means you are ready for a meditation retreat, either in the company of others or on your own. A number of traditions, both Christian and Buddhist, operate retreat centres or monasteries where retreats can be taken, and you can contact them for details. But a 'retreat' can mean a number of different things. It can mean a study weekend where periods of meditation are interspersed with teaching and discussion sessions. Or it can mean a period of time where, though you are in the company of others, you are left to decide for yourself when and how you want to practice. Or it can be an intensive silent retreat with a full timetable of meditation sessions starting early in the morning and going on into the evening (as many as ten or twelve hours a day in total), with short breaks only for silent meals or for work periods.

If you decide to go on a retreat, be sure you know what you are letting yourself in for before you go. Don't take on too much too soon. All retreats demand a degree of discipline, but you should feel able to sit for several twenty or 30-minute sessions a day before you attempt even the least onerous of them. If you have a physical disability, allowances will of course be made, and in any case there is no compulsion placed upon you to do anything, but if you are attending a retreat then those running it will naturally prefer you to conform to the pattern which they have laid down.

The great value of a retreat is that it allows you, through the intensity of your practice, to develop concentration, tranquillity and insight more rapidly than you would otherwise be able to do. In the first day or two of a retreat you may feel nothing is happening, but by the third day you may find yourself in a still state which penetrates both your meditation and the periods between meditation, a still state where everything opens out and the boundaries between yourself and your environment dissolve, and you feel in touch with some source of intuitive wisdom inside yourself. (You may even feel something of the heightened state of bliss to which experienced meditators refer, but that is another matter!)

However, though retreats are a great help, they are no substitute for regular daily practice. Some people return from a retreat feeling they have at last made progress; then, struck by the 'dullness' of routine sitting, they cease to do anything until the next retreat. This is a major mistake. Retreats are there to supplement your daily practice, not to replace it. They are times for taking stock, for getting a further perspective on where you are, for exploring more fully the potential of what it is you are doing when you sit to practise. But when all is said and done they are a withdrawal from everyday life, from the marketplace in which you have to earn your living. The real test of where you are is your daily routine, and the extent to which you can not only find a space within it for mediation, but can apply the insights supplied by meditation to your 'ordinary' life of work, leisure and relationships.

CONCLUSION

Some journeys have a definite destination, and when you arrive at it you know you have arrived. Other journeys are different. You set off not knowing quite where you are going or why, but knowing it is a journey you want to take. Or a journey which, for reasons which you cannot even explain to yourself, you feel you must take. You carry with you the few things you think you are going to need, and then find bit by bit that most of these can be left behind too.

Meditation is the second kind of journey. Now that you have come this far, some of the scenery is familiar to you. There are landmarks which you recognize, and which open out and welcome you. There are highways and byways. Sometimes you seem to be going back in the direction from which you came, at other times you seem to be covering a great deal of ground very quickly. There are surprises. Unexpected experiences, some of them encouraging, some of them apparently disconcerting. And always in the distance there are the far hills and the trees on the horizon.

It is possible that the journey of meditation has no end. That the path, like space and time, is infinite. Or it is possible that the destination is yourself, and that you and that infinity are one. No matter. Concentrate upon travelling with hope and with courage, and your meditation will not fail you. I wish you peace and joy on your journey, and the kindness of friends as your blessing.

REFERENCES AND FURTHER READING

A number of authorities are mentioned or quoted in the text. Below is a selection of their work and other books which will help you in your study of meditation. Some explanatory details are given on each.

Arnold, E. *The Light of Asia*, Routledge & Kegan Paul, 1971. A long poem on the life, character and philosophy of the Buddha; full of profound insights beautifully expressed.

Bancroft, A. *Zen: Direct Pointing at Reality*, Thames and Hudson, 1979. A beautifully illustrated survey of many Zen practices, including walking meditation.

Blofeld, J. *Mantras: Sacred Words of Power*, Unwin, 1977. Available as a Mandela paperback, this is one of the best short introductions to the meaning and power of the mantra.

Blyth, R. H. *A History of Haiku* (2 vols), Hokuseido Press, 1964. An excellent, definitive survey of haiku poetry. Published in Tokyo, it is still in print but may be difficult to obtain.

Carrington, P. 'Managing meditation in clinical practice', in M. West (ed.) *The Psychology of Meditation*, Oxford University Press, 1987. A thorough survey of many of the medical and psychological benefits of meditation.

Chögyam, Ngakpa *Journey into Vastness*, Element Books, 1988. Excellent introduction to Tibetan meditational practices, including shi-ne.

Conze, E. *Buddhist Meditation*, Unwin, 1972. One of the most readily available sources for the Buddha's own teaching on vipassana.

Cooper, J. C. *An Illustrated Encyclopedia of Traditional Symbols*, Thames and Hudson, 1978. A must for all those interested in symbols and their significance. A scholarly but highly readable work, profusely illustrated, and now available as a large-format paperback.

Eliot, T. S. *Collected Poems 1909–1962*, Faber & Faber, 1963. Of all modern Western poets, Eliot had the surest grasp of mystical experience, and combined an understanding of both Western and Eastern spirituality. Available in paperback.

French, R. M. (translator) *The Way of a Pilgrim*, SPCK, 1942. A classic of Christian meditational literature using the Jesus prayer. Available in paperback.

Govinda, Lama Anagarika *Creative Meditation and Multi-dimensional Consciousness*, Unwin, 1977. Available as a Mandala paperback. Not an easy book, but richly rewarding. Deals with colours as well as mantras and mandalas.

Herrigel, E. *Zen in the Art of Archery*, Routledge, 1953. A classic, as perfect as a Zen painting or a haiku poem. In R. F. C. Hull's beautiful translation from the German, the book says more in each sentence than most books say in their whole length. Continuously in print and now available as an Arkana paperback.

Jung, C. *Memories, Dreams, Reflections*, Fontana, 1967. The autobiography of the Western psychologist most in tune with the psychological value of meditation. Now available as a Fount paperback.

Mascaro, J. (translator) *The Dhammapada*, Penguin, 1973. One of the great spiritual classics of world literature.

McDonald, K. *How to Meditate*, Wisdom, 1984. A very practical guide to the use, among other things, of the visualization of the Buddha–or other spiritual teachers–in meditation.

Sekida, K. (translator) *Two Zen Classics: Mumonkan and Hekiganroku*, Weatherhill, 1977. Two of the most mind-baffling collections of koans. Perhaps the ultimate experience in Zen literature.

Sheng-Yen, Master *Getting the Buddha Mind*, Dharma Drum Publications, 1982. The teachings of a modern Ch'an master during a meditation retreat.

Simonton, O.C. Mathews-Simonton, S. and Creighton, J.L. *Getting Well Again*, Bantam Books, 1980. An excellent introduction to the use of visualizations for healing and health.

Suzuki, D. T. *Essays in Zen Buddhism* (3 Vols), Rider, 1953. One of the best of the many publications produced by the man who first made Zen comprehensible to the West.

Van de Wetering, J. *A Glimpse of Nothingness*, Routledge, 1979. First-hand account of experiences in an American Zen community.

INDEX

117